MICROMASTERY

MICROMASTERY

Learn Small, Learn Fast, and Unlock
Your Potential to Achieve Anything

Robert Twigger

A TarcherPerigee Book

tarcherperigee

An imprint of Penguin Random House LLC
375 Hudson Street
New York, New York 10014

First published in Great Britain by Penguin Life, an imprint of Penguin Random House UK 2017

Drawings and photographs by the author

TarcherPerigee with tp colophon is a registered trademark of Penguin Random House LLC.

Most TarcherPerigee books are available at special quantity discounts for
bulk purchase for sales promotions, premiums, fund-raising, and educational needs.
Special books or book excerpts also can be created to fit specific needs.
For details, write: SpecialMarkets@penguinrandomhouse.com.

Library of Congress Cataloging-in-Publication Data

Names: Twigger, Robert, 1964– author.
Title: Micromastery : learn small, learn fast, and unlock your potential to
achieve anything / Robert Twigger.
Description: New York, New York : TarcherPerigee, 2018. | Originally
published: London : Penguin Life, 2017.
Identifiers: LCCN 2017039317 (print) | LCCN 2017056050 (ebook) |
ISBN 9780525504306 (ebook) | ISBN 9780143132325 (paperback)
Subjects: LCSH: Cognitive psychology. | Ability. | Expertise. | BISAC:
PSYCHOLOGY / Cognitive Psychology. | SELF-HELP / Personal Growth / Success. |
SELF-HELP / Personal Growth / Happiness.
Classification: LCC BF201 (ebook) | LCC BF201 .T85 2018 (print) |
DDC 153.1/52—dc23
LC record available at https://lccn.loc.gov/2017039317

Printed in the United States of America
1 3 5 7 9 10 8 6 4 2

The memory of Rabia Basri 714–801

The creative scientist needs an artistic imagination.

Max Planck, 1918 winner of the Nobel Prize in Physics

Contents

Micromastery   1

    What is Micromastery?   3

    Inside a Micromastery   16

    Dynamic Learning   27

    Locate Hidden Micromasteries
       (They Are Everywhere)   32

    Help Yourself   40

    Multiple Micromastery and Synergy   65

    Polymathic Paradise   76

    Creativity Explosion   83

Micromastery Central   91

  1 **Do a Line Sketch That Looks Creditable**   93

  2 **Do an Eskimo Roll**   96

  3 **Find the Depth of a Well or a Deep Hole**   101

  4 **Chop Through a Log (or Even a Tree)**   104

  5 **Learn How to Climb a Rope**   107

  6 **Surf Standing Up**   111

  7 **Talk for Fifteen Minutes about Any Subject**   115

  8 **Lay a Brick Wall**   118

Contents

9 Write Dialogue 122

10 Make a Clay Skull 125

11 Bake Excellent Artisan Bread 128

12 Make a Sword Hum Through the Air 132

13 Make String from Nettles 135

14 Sing Solo, Even If You Are Tone Deaf 138

15 Master the Bench Press 141

16 Learn "La Marseillaise" 144

17 Do a Soccer *Elastico* 146

18 Build a Superstack of Wood 150

19 Develop Film Using Coffee and Salt 154

20 Do a High-Speed Getaway J-Turn 157

21 Make Sushi . . . That Actually Looks
and Tastes Like Sushi 160

22 Tell a Story That Will Enthrall Any Child 163

23 Immobilize Someone with an Aikido Hold 165

24 Juggle Four Balls 168

25 Master the Three-Card Trick 171

26 Grow a Bonsai Tree 175

27 Make a Perfect Soufflé Every Time 178

28 Make a Perfect Cube of Wood 181

29 Mix a Delightful Daiquiri 185

30 Walk the Tango Walk 188

31 Make Fire by Rubbing Two Sticks Together 191

32 Make Your Handwriting Beautiful 194

33 Micromaster Bargaining 197

34 Hone a Kitchen Knife So That It Is Razor Sharp 200

35 Lead a Small Group in the Wilderness 203

36 Learn to Read Japanese in Three Hours 206

37 Become a Street Photographer   208

38 Brew Delicious Craft Beer   211

39 Make Your Own Shirt   214

Micromaster Your Life   217

Permission to Be Interested   219

Your Many Selves   223

Punk Micromastery   230

Micromastery vs Global Pessimism   233

The BIG, BIGGER, BIGGEST Picture   238

Micromastery

What is Micromastery?

Start with the egg, not the chicken

YouTube has clips of *The Great Egg Race*, a long-running TV show in the 1980s, hosted by an amiable German-born egghead called Dr. Heinz Wolff. Like a forerunner and more inventive version of *Scrapheap Challenge*, contestants had to build a gadget with limited resources to meet the challenge set out at the start of the show. In the early series all the tasks involved an egg that mustn't be broken, the first task being to make a machine to transport an egg the farthest distance possible using only paper clips, card, and rubber bands. It was such a simple idea, yet it gave rise to incredibly inventive machines. And it all started with an egg, something rather small and humble.

Life can be overwhelming. We want to do as much as we can, see the world, learn new things—and it can all get a bit too much. I reached a point in my life when I felt that I could no longer be interested in *everything*. I had to shut some of life out, and I didn't like that. I was living under the assumption—the false assumption, as it turned out—that to know anything worthwhile took years of study, so I might as well forget it.

But something inside me rebelled. I still wanted to learn new things and make new things. They didn't have to be big things—I was happy to leave that till later. Start small, start humble.

Start with an egg.

So I was thinking about how long it would take to learn how to cook really well. I recalled a chef telling me that the real test is doing something simple—like making a perfect omelet. Everything you know about cooking comes out in this simple dish. So I decided to switch the order around. Instead of spending 10,000 hours learning the basics of cookery and then showing my expertise in omelet making, I'd start with just making an omelet.

I really focused on making that omelet. I separated it from the basic need that cooking usually fulfills—filling my stomach—so that it now occupied a special, singular place in my life. It had become a micromastery.

A micromastery is a self-contained unit of doing, complete in itself but connected to a greater field. You can perfect that single thing or move on to bigger things—or you can do both. A micromastery is repeatable and has a success payoff. It is pleasing in and of itself. You can experiment with the micromastery because it has a certain elasticity—you can bend it and stretch it, and as you do you learn in a three-dimensional way that appeals to the multisensory neurons in our brain.

It's the way we learn as kids. You never absorb all the fundamentals straight away—you learn one cool thing, then another. You learn a 360 on a skateboard or how to make a crystal radio. My father was a teacher, and he hoped to encourage me when he told me that he would buy me the parts to make a transistor radio when I could explain how a transistor worked. My interest died immediately. I knew how to make the radio and have fun with it, but having to explain it was something difficult, adult, and alien. And wrong. (Dad, I forgive you.)

Hungarian psychologist Mihaly Csikszentmihalyi has written extensively about "flow"—a state in which time seems to be suspended because our interest and involvement in what we're doing are so great.* A micromastery, because it is repeatable without being repetitious, has all the elements that allow us to enter a flow state, which produces great contentment and enhances physical and mental health.

Learning a micromastery doesn't commit you in that deadening way that buying a beginner's textbook does. By its limited nature, it gives you permission to remain interested in the world. It doesn't mean you have to commit to doing that thing for what feels like forever, and at the same time it spares you any worries that you've wasted your time.

Do you know the feeling of doing an introductory course on something, which you give up on, and then a few years later you try to tell others what you learned, but you can't remember? A micromastery isn't like that. It's with you forever—and it's nice to have something to show others. For instance if you learn a martial art you need something to shut people up with when they say, "Go on, show us a move."

A micromastery has a structure that connects in a crucial way

* Mihaly Csikszentmihalyi, *Flow: The Psychology of Optimal Experience* (Harper-Perennial, 1990).

to important elements in the greater field it is a part of. It reveals relationships and balances in the elements of the task that mere words and explanation, textbook-style, cannot. Its repeatability and gameability—people like that omelet, ask for another, you start to aim higher—turn it into a self-teaching mechanism, where experimentation within certain defined limits greatly increases your learning.

But let's get back to starting with an egg—or two.

A chef gave me the tip about using the fork to bulk up the omelet. I kept practicing. I went online and found more tips. Then a French woman told me about separating the yolk from the white, which allows your omelet to double in thickness and softness. When it's served, people simply go: "Wow!"

This is what I call the "entry trick." Every micromastery has one. It is a way, in one stroke, to elevate your performance at that task and get an immediate payoff—a rush of rewarding neurochemicals, which is a nice warm feeling.

In some micromasteries, the entry trick is huge, an integral part of the whole thing. In others it just gives you enough of a push to get you going. There are lots of big-shot learners out there boasting of their ability to master foreign languages, get calculus down, or absorb C++ programming, but they all seem to miss this point. Learning must not be like school; it must not be boring. It doesn't need to be silly fun, but it mustn't be deadening or dull or too hard. The entry trick, in one fell swoop, sweeps all that away.

A great entry trick is used in stone balancing. Maybe you've seen some stone-sculptor type doing it at the beach. It looks like magic—rounded rocks and mini-boulders balancing on each other in a seemingly impossible way. The first time I saw such a sculpture I thought it had to have glue or metal rods inside it . . . and then I watched a small boy knock it over. When I attempted to help rebuild it, the sculptor showed me the entry trick.

(The pictures are some I made myself on the beach, later, when I had learned how to do it.)

You can balance any stone at all, but you must find *three raised bits* close together on one side of the supporting stone—three

bumps, three nodules, or even three grains. They can be tiny, almost invisible. In fact the smaller they are, the better it looks. These three bumps act as a flat triangle for another curved object to fit into. That's how you make these crazy balances work. People look for flat bits on the stones to make them stand on each other, but that doesn't work because nothing in nature is really flat.

Stone balancing is not only fun, but also a perfect form of micromastery. It is complete in itself, but it could also lead you further into the greater world of sculpture and outdoor art—should you want to go there.

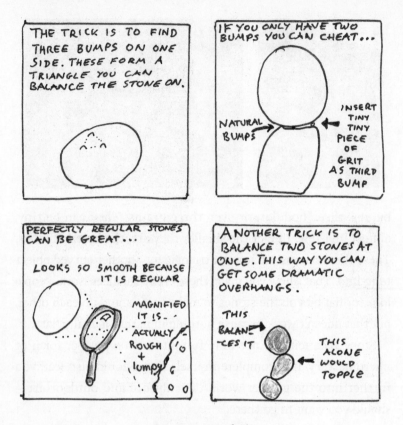

Anyone can do it

We envy the person who has a perfect French accent, who can roll a kayak, perform a double or even triple integral in math or compose a poem that isn't laughable; who can draw something well, do a magic trick, or lay a brick wall that doesn't fall down. These are perceived as hard things to learn that signify a greater mastery of the field concerned. But with micromastery you start with the test piece and then—and only then—do you go back upstream to explore more.

Why?

Because the biggest reasons for not achieving anything are giving up, failing to gain momentum, and becoming distracted. You may imagine you are tough and self-contained, but we all need a payoff as soon as we start learning. Especially if it's been a while since we tried anything new. If you don't have microsuccesses along the way you'll lose heart and give up, especially if you are learning something on your own.

Rapid learning techniques, intensive courses, and shortcuts are all very well, but if you haven't got a show-offable product at the end you'll give up. It's no good telling your friends and family that you have a broad knowledge of the background of math or a working acquaintanceship with magic tricks. "Come on," they'll say, "show us something now!"

Having a micromastery gives you something to boast about (as loudly or as quietly as you like). It gives something to connect you to others, and earn that all-important feedback. No man, woman, or child is an island—and yet we are taught as if we are solitary brain-blobs who just suck up knowledge until one miraculous day we are "masters," "qualified," "ready to teach," or some other spurious designation. We are not like that. Humans want to pass on what they have learned straight away, not five years later.

Ask the experts

Those who have mastered their field are often a great source of insight, and I have talked to many such experts to produce the micromasteries outlined in this book. They often approach their subject from a perspective I'd never have thought about.

When I spoke to former England Schools rugby player and coach of the Nigerian Sevens team Rupert Seldon, he didn't, as I'd expected, suggest spin passing as a micromastery of his sport. He preferred the drop kick, a more technical skill. A Madame Tussauds sculptor told me how modeling a human skull from clay, or even Plasticine, is a micromastery that starts you on the path to producing lifelike sculptures. He explained how you see the "skull beneath the skin" when you look at someone you want to model.

Usually, I combine asking an expert with my own research. Having learned traditional martial arts in Japan, I already knew that the Japanese use kata and self-contained exercises—micromasteries—in most of their teaching.

The Japanese approach to learning—be it martial arts, the tea ceremony, or calligraphy—is different from Western methods of teaching. In the West the tacit assumption is that you either start very young, possibly driven by obsessive parents, or you have an innate talent. Teaching is conceived as a kind of coaching, and if you haven't got the talent you're considered a lost cause.

The Japanese know that talent is rather overrated. More important is your attitude toward learning. So their method of teaching assumes that everyone can learn—whatever their initial level of skill. Instead of hoping that students "pick it up" by osmosis, as is done in the West, micromastery routines are devised so that everyone, even the apparently talentless, can learn.

Drawing is a good case in point. Lots of people swear they "can't draw," but that usually means they can't draw a picture that looks like someone. This is like saying you can't cook when you haven't ever read a recipe book or bought any ingredients. You have to start a few stages further back, with something simple, something humble.

Shoo Rayner—who has illustrated hundreds of children's books—has a website dedicated to helping people learn to draw. When I talked to him he emphasized that all objects can be reduced to simple shapes—cubes, spheres, and cylinders—and these can be even further reduced to lines and curves. He said, "If you can draw a line, you can draw." The next step is to draw straight lines and then curved lines—which is where Zen circles come in.

The thing I like to look for first is the entry trick, the piece of insider information that elevates your initial attempt above that of the average first-timer and shows you the way into the micromastery. With circle-drawing there are not one but three tricks to get you going.

Holding your pencil, pen, or, ideally, brush midway down its handle is the single easiest way to improve drawing. The further you can move your gripping finger and thumb from the point, the easier you will find it. There will be a miraculous improvement over the crabbed, nib-pinching style many of us have developed from our schooldays. Holding the pen higher up will improve not only all your drawing, but also your handwriting.

You can then try lifting your hand off the table and using your whole arm, rather than just your hand isolated at the wrist, to make the circle. The neurological reason for doing this is that a greater area of the brain is being stimulated, so the learning is deeper and, ultimately, a greater refinement of movement is possible. Classical guitarist David Leisner claimed that he recovered from focal hand dystonia, the repetitive-strain illness that often affects guitarists, by retraining using his *whole arm* instead of just his wrist. This not only aided his recovery, but also, amazingly, improved his performances.

Another entry trick, beloved by signwriters who need to get very accurate curves and circles, is to rest your drawing hand on your fist. Make the circle by using a combination of moving the drawing arm while also moving the fist to guide it. You can experiment with how much you move the supporting fist.

Seeing the world in terms of micromasteries makes anything seem possible. Fancy bookbinding? Yoga? Tap dancing or tank driving? All have their micromasteries. It's very liberating—you no longer have to feel trapped in whatever your day job happens to be. You will start, in a small way—a humble way—to get your life back from the idea the world seems to push on us that we should do just one thing all our lives.

Inside a Micromastery

When you've seen someone start a fire in the woods using just their hands and a wooden drill, or cook a perfect omelet, or lead you in a snappy tango across the dance floor, you don't forget it easily. These skillful activities all look hard, but the difficulty is made manageable by using the structure necessary to achieve them.

Every micromastery has a precise structure:

1. **The entry trick**
2. **The rub-pat barrier**
3. **Background support**
4. **The payoff**
5. **Repeatability**
6. **Experimental possibilities**

Knowing the structure helps you learn the micromastery, and also helps you identify other things as potential micromasteries. It enables you, on approaching a new subject of study, to identify for yourself the parts of it that can be micromastered, thus speeding up the learning and increasing your chances of sticking with it.

1. The entry trick

We've seen how the trick is your way in, your leg up. The entry trick overcomes the barriers to getting started that all new micromasteries present. Some of these have to do with confidence and familiarity, and some have to do with giving the right amount of emphasis to each part of the process. The entry trick is a quick way to get a basic grip on the matter. You may, in the end, not need to use it—but at first it's your best friend.

It could be a simple methodological change like holding the pen higher, or separating the egg yolk from the white before making an omelet. Or it could be setting out to focus on one area of training—the trick to standing up on a surfboard is to practice jumping up on to the board on your living-room floor. When doing a 360-degree turn on a skateboard you turn the eyes and head first—and the body follows. The trick could be a number of things to pay special attention to: in making fire with a bow drill you need everything to be bone dry and as far off the ground as is practicable—it's amazing how moisture congregates close to the ground. (Don't worry if this seems like a bit of a rush through some intriguing micromasteries—we'll come back and deal with them all in Part Two of this book.)

The trick is what sucks you in and then suckers you in—you tell yourself that if you know the trick, you can already do it. Knowing this helps the hours of practice if not fly by, then at least pass with tolerable speed.

Some micromasteries have several tricks—we saw that in drawing Zen circles you can change the pen grip or rest one hand on top of the other. Some have a rather subtle trick. In street photography it is simply "get closer"—with this single focus your photographs will improve exponentially.

You might reach a point when you discover that you don't need the trick any more. But it's done its work by then—pulling you in enough for you to perfect the micromastery.

2. The rub-pat, or countervailing skill, barrier

Many of the tricks which are used to get a head start connect to the rub-pat barrier (also known as the countervailing skill barrier) at the heart of micromastery. This is the point where you will find two skills needed for the task start to work against each other. The name comes from the difficulty of both rubbing your stomach and patting your head at the same time. At first sight it appears easy; then you try, and find it . . . almost impossible. Finally, you focus more on one than the other, keeping one going and then bringing the other in slowly until you succeed.

We tend to think of skills acquisition in a simplistic way. You just pile one on top of the other, don't you? But skills can either help the mastery of further skills or actually *retard* such mastery. We think of something complex like learning to drive as a task of coordinating several skills. But it is also useful to go through each skill and see how it actually messes with the others. Changing gear interferes with steering—it doesn't help it in any way. Better to perfect each independently rather than suffer the consequences of doing them poorly together.

The rub-pat barrier is where this kind of contradiction is most heightened. It's the highest hurdle you'll have to leap when learning something new. If you can clear it, you're more than halfway home. Isolating the countervailing skills is a very useful exercise. It takes the mystery and scariness out of learning something new. It allows you to break a new subject down into manageable chunks.

In any attempt to learn something worthwhile you'll hit rub-pat skill barriers: this task of coordinating different pathways in the brain. But being able to shift focus isn't always easy: often the task overwhelms us and we panic and give up. "I just don't get it!" we plead. Fast learners unconsciously focus on each element in turn when they learn new things that seem hard. It can make them seem a little pedantic, but you cannot build awareness if you hurry. You need to be "outside time." (I find if I allow two hours for any learning session I quickly forget about time and things start to flow. But if I assign less time I begin to rush.) The entry trick also helps here—it lessens the impact of conflict of skills and assists in balancing them.

Just knowing that this barrier exists will make it easier to conquer the micromastery. It will focus your efforts.

Back to the Zen circle. The rub-pat barrier here is not too bad—though it stumps some people who have been convinced (or convinced themselves) they "can't draw." The two elements that vie with each other and need to be balanced are the slow pace required to make a detailed and careful line versus the speed and flair needed to make a good curve. Slow down too much and your circle will look like an amoeba. Speed up too much and you'll get an egg-shaped flourish with sticking out ends like the hair on a cartoon character's head.

Some micromasteries have low rub-pat barriers. They are quite easy to get started on. In stone balancing, once you know the entry trick and have a good supply of stones, the rub-pat barrier becomes apparent only when you realize that the crazier the balance, the harder it is to build on. You need to coordinate spotting tiny bumps and balance spots with visualizing an entire tower of stones. A really good balance spot for three stones may throw a five-stone tower out of kilter. Moving the stones back and forth, so that you have a subunit that balances, before making that balance on top of another stone really is like rubbing your stomach and patting your head.

For others, the rub-pat barrier is the main obstacle to doing the thing at all. Juggling has an obviously high rub-pat barrier. You need to be able to throw and catch with each hand pretty much at the same time. The trick is to focus on throwing for a while, then focus on catching. By separating and building the skills you grow the neural pathways involved so that you are better able to operate on autopilot.

If you like, assign a score to how much you are focusing on one rather than the other, or your competence level at each skill. Maybe you are a "9" on throwing and only "2" on catching. Numbering the inner elements of a skill (worked out at length in Timothy Gallwey's excellent *Inner Game* series of books) is a great way to take the pressure off trying harder at both skills at once. When we try too hard to crack the rub-pat barrier it usually just results in frustration. Better to keep coming back to it and continually revising the numbers assigned to each countervailing skill.

The Eskimo roll, the technique used by paddlers to right a capsized kayak while remaining inside it, may look scary at first. But

the rub-pat barrier of using the hips to flip up the boat in conjunc-
tion with the hands can be easily separated. You can rock the boat
up against a dock while holding on to the firm surface and practice using the hips in this controlled way. By identifying the
rub-pat barrier in advance you can offset a lot of its terror.

Going to the level higher than you want ultimately to achieve is
connected to an aikido training skill called *hajime* training. In
hajime (which means "begin" in Japanese) you simply do each
technique as fast as possible. It doesn't matter how badly you do
it as long as you go at top speed. This forces you into a flow state
and makes conscious thinking impossible. You then alternate this
with doing the technique as slowly as possible. The variation
builds awareness and loads the basic countervailing skill deep into
the brain.

Performing countervailing skills means using two parts of your
brain at once. The brain likes to do one thing at a time if you
insist on being conscious about it, but if you can let go of thinking,
you'll find you can master very complex skills that require using
multiple parts of the brain simultaneously. Thinking—by which I
mean verbalizing in your head and following these instructions—
is a sure-fire way to look like a dummy. The faster you can get a
feel for something and just do it, the better.

Guidelines can be useful, of course. When you learn to drive,
instructors sometimes put marks on the car's back window which
you can line up with the edge of the curb in order to parallel park
perfectly every time. After a while, though, you get to sense
exactly where you are. You can do it by eye. This always seems
amazing to newcomers to an art, but actually we are excellent at
doing things by eye. In the nineteenth century wheelwrights

would make perfect wheels not by measuring, but by using their highly attuned sense of natural measurement alone. Doing it by eye means trusting our own ability to use a countervailing skill.

3. Background support

Before making any attempt at learning a micromastery you need to give yourself the best chance to succeed. You need good equipment or tools, time, and an open mind. You should not be in a hurry. Even think about making use of downtime (the comedian and actor Steve Martin learned the banjo by placing one in every room in his house, including the bathroom). You need to remove all obstacles in your way.

Sometimes the right bit of gear is the one that helps demolish the rub-pat barrier. In freediving, for example, the rub-pat barrier is balancing the rate of descent against pressure in the ears. Go too fast and your ears will hurt like hell; go too slow and you won't get anywhere. For many the breakthrough is aided by a simple piece of gear: Doc's Proplugs, also used by musicians, which let water in slowly through a small hole, thus equalizing the pressure more smoothly and, incidentally, reducing the chance of ear infections. In street photography the rub-pat barrier is speed versus shake/blur—this can be offset by having a small camera with very fast focus.

In any case, having the right gear means the right gear *for you*. The gear that inspires you to keep practicing again and again. In film photography some are drawn to the off-the-wall use of instant coffee and vitamin C as a developing agent—yes, it works. Although it's more hassle than using a commercial developer, it's the right gear in the sense that it's fun and intriguing.

For Zen circles it helps to have a pen you really like using. Artists and illustrators tend to have their personal favorites. Shoo Rayner likes to use a Rotring pen and writer/illustrator Dan Price uses a Japanese Sakura fiber-tip. I've grown to love the Pentel brush pen used by manga artists—it seems to make Zen circles even more fun to do.

But background support isn't just about gear—it includes the environment and the people around you. My daughter was almost ready to give up the guitar, but we found another teacher and she not only learned far faster, but is now also really keen. The right teacher makes a huge difference. They don't have to be brilliant— they just have to be able to make you want to do more of whatever you are interested in. Just as doctors aid the body to heal itself, teachers redirect our attention to help us teach ourselves.

4. The payoff

All micromasteries are structured with some kind of success payoff—it's what makes you *want* to repeat them. The fact that the micromastery looks hard—juggling, proving Pythagoras using origami—gives you an incentive and, whether your motivation is to look good or meet the inner challenge (or both), there needs to be a clear and unequivocal state of achievable success in a micromastery. That's why cooking is not a micromastery but making an omelet is; why driving isn't but performing a handbrake turn is; even why paddling a canoe isn't but doing an Eskimo roll really is.

There are degrees of sharpness and definition to the success involved. The sharper and brighter it is, the more applause you usually get. We all need attention—it's a vital form of human nourishment. In evolutionary terms humans require others for survival throughout life, not just in infancy. We find it far easier to survive as part of a group than as an individual in the wild, and getting attention from others means we are a member of the gang. Of course, you need to be weaned off needing more attention than is healthy, but you still need some. Even the attention we give ourselves is a personal payoff—the nice warm feeling that we've done it, even if no one else knows about it.

For some, the public payoff can be a strong motivating force. Coach and creativity teacher Steve Chapman announces his challenges publicly and uses the threat of humiliation to drive him forward. Laziness and distraction are overcome by fear—a clever case of using a negative quality to defeat other negative qualities.

Simply being *more useful* can be a great motivator and give you the payoff you need. If you can cook great food, be entertaining, be more fun, able to fix things—that is reward enough.

A micromastery leaves you feeling that you've achieved something—however tiny. I've found when drawing Zen circles that I often cover an entire page but try to keep them from overlapping. The bubble effect adds to my payoff.

5. Repeatability

You have to be able to repeat a micromastery endlessly, so it cannot be too boring or inflexible or unchanging. Most importantly, you have to be able to get better at doing it. You repeat and repeat and watch yourself improve. It's really quite astonishing.

I have set myself the micromastery of always drawing the cup, spoon, and saucer whenever I go into a coffee shop. Sometimes I do it painstakingly, a real still life. Other times I'm in a diabolical hurry and dash the sketch off in under a minute. It doesn't matter, as long as I keep doing it, keep repeating this simple task. I can feel myself getting more confident, and I am seeing better—seeing more of what has always been there. Because even when I'm in a rush I'm not in that semi-panicked state of mind, which is part fear of getting it wrong and part fear that I won't finish it for some reason. These fears, a kind of small and personal performance fear, can dog even our most private and unpressured attempts to create or try something new. By having a set time and a repeatable format you can drive away those devils of self-doubt.

The holy grail of marketers is to make something "gameable," which means repeatable and addictive by virtue of having a surprise ending. If it is too predictable we get bored. No omelet is quite the same as another, just as it is with a bout of juggling or a Zen circle— there is a chance the next one will be better. Herein lies gameability. For this to occur it must be easy to repeat the micromastery—novel writing is not a micromastery, but hundred-word flash-fiction writing is. Climbing Everest isn't, but scaling your local climbing wall is.

6. Experimental possibilities

A micromastery is like a miniature lab, a place to try countless experiments that will further your knowledge and lead you deeper into the subject in question. Experimentation is not the province of science; science merely appropriates this deeply human form of curiosity.

Through experimentation you can give added zest to repeatability. You can improve exponentially, achieving something that would take eons of straight, repetitive "getting better" practice. I decided long ago to micromaster the J-stroke for a canoe, used when you are at the back of the boat or alone in a Canadian canoe. The "J" describes the path of the paddle through the water, as seen from above. I read up on it and started using it every time I went out on the nearby river. I couldn't really get it. Then I had a conversation with an expert, my cousin Simon, who is a former Olympic team canoeist. He told me with admirable self-deprecation that mostly he did a kind of C-stroke. I got it straight away—he had given me permission to experiment. Instead of trying to follow the instructions by the letter, I should have been having fun—doing C-, L-, J-, and maybe even Z-strokes. I got better immediately, finding my own way to a more powerful paddling stroke.

Every micromastery is there to be twisted, turned, done back to front, messed up, and generally had fun with. It's the way you learn the variables—how far they can be pushed and how they affect each other. One of the grave errors of learning-outcome-type teaching is that it moves too swiftly for endless experimenting and mucking about. Keep drawing circles, making skulls out of clay, doing wheelies on your bike—forget learning outcomes and come out and actually learn.

Dynamic Learning

Alexander Hopkins is a world-class maker of medieval-style musical instruments. He started when he was in his late teens, before he had any kind of training. He knew he wanted to make a violin so he bought a book about instrument making, but he couldn't understand it. It just didn't make sense. In a fit of frustration he decided to make a violin using just whatever he knew, copying pictures and hoping for the best. It was terrible. But then when he went back to the book he understood it. He made another violin, and this time it was really rather good.

Books convey static learning, which is why highly practical and physical activities—such as martial arts—can't be learned from them. However, once you know something about martial arts you can use a book to enhance your skills.

Static learning is about following a sequence of steps. Dynamic learning is about the relationship between the steps and how much emphasis to give each one. As we've already discussed, we learn, essentially, by watching others—this is how we grasp the correct emphasis to apply to each step of what we are doing.

Alexander Hopkins had no one to watch, but by making a rough version of a violin he learned the rudiments of how much importance to attach to each part of the making process. In a sense, this first attempt was like a micromastery—a small nugget of dynamic learning.

Confidence, center, balance

In addition to knowing the elements of a micromastery's structure, it's helpful to look at its dynamic relationship to confidence, center, and balance, which I find makes the whole task more real to me.

I learned this from eighth-dan aikido master Jacques Payet. He teaches something very simple yet powerful: when you find where your physical center should be in any attack or defense, your balance improves. With improved balance your confidence improves. When you have more confidence, you feel more sure of your center. It's a virtuous circle of improvement. It works the opposite way too—when your confidence is shaken you can't find your center, so your balance goes, which weakens your confidence and your performance declines.

Finding your center when learning a micromastery can give you an injection of confidence and make it easier to comprehend—it is the place around which it all revolves. Obviously, this is more significant with some than others. *What is the center of making an omelet?* sounds rather Zen, but maybe just thinking about it will help you improve. In some micromasteries it might help to think of the right stance, the right position, the right setup, but, out of all of these, one thing will be of focal importance. With an omelet it is the heat of the pan—which is a function both of the stove's power, the kind of pan, and the type of fat used. The center is where you focus awareness. The center of the seemingly simple act of chopping wood is the ax handle, not the ax head—you feel the weight through the handle and react to that.

Finding your center can be literal—as in surfing or dancing—or it can be metaphorical. It is almost always located at the rub-pat barrier. In drawing Zen circles, the balance point, as we've seen, is between the need to be accurate and the need to be smooth. The center is how you hold your arm, how it is positioned to address both these needs.

Identify the effort hotspots

My ears were dribbling water. My eyes stung with chlorine. I had that sick feeling you get after ingesting too much water that too many people—and canoes—have been in. I had been rolling for hours (probably just one hour but it felt like ten) and I had yet actually to do one successful standard Eskimo roll in my canoe. I was learning the hard way.

There is a hard way and an easy, or at least easier, way to learn everything. And the easier way embraces all the so-called "cheats" and tricks needed to get you learning fast. Micromastery aims to make learning easier, not harder, since the biggest obstacle to learning is giving up because it takes too long.

When I started to learn how to do an Eskimo roll, the standard way to recover from a kayak capsizing without having to leave the boat, I was a teenager doing a scout course at the local swimming pool. The instruction was verbose and we had nothing to connect it to. We saw our teacher do only a single roll in one of the tiny snub-nosed kayaks. We didn't know how much effort to put into each step of the technique, so we were overexerting in all of them and tiring ourselves out. This is why many people fail. They don't know the effort hotspots.

These hotspots can be identified in every activity, so you can learn how to *throttle back* and conserve energy when necessary, and *blast out* when you need to.

Rope climbing is an instructive example. The trick with rope climbing is to use your arm strength only sparingly. If you don't, you'll never move more than a few feet upward. As with all forms of climbing, your feet do the real work. With a thick gym rope you can get enough grip by pressing the rope between your ankles. With thinner ropes, imagine an "S" shaped loop with one foot in the top pushing down on the rope as it goes over the other foot in the lower rope loop. You learn to stand up on the rope with all the weight on your feet. You then move your hands up and simply dangle. The only arm strength involved is that which is needed to hang from the rope, not climb it. You then bring your feet up, lock them again on to the rope, and again stand high—your knees doing the raising of your weight.

You have to concentrate your arm strength in the small bursts of activity as you raise your knees. The quicker you do this, the less arm strength you need. The more coordinated you are, the less arm and finger strength you need. By finding the effort hotspot you succeed.

There is a similar need for a burst of concentrated, coordinated strength in surfing. Riding a moving board isn't that hard—once you are standing on it. The hard part is getting up in a quick and easy move before the wave runs out or the board overbalances. If you go out to surf without isolating and practicing the single-board standing move, you'll probably get tired and cold before you have a chance to use it. And then you'll never learn.

In all these things—the Eskimo roll, rope climbing, and surfing—the effort hotspot lies in the rub-pat barrier at the heart of each activity. And because each one requires a certain strength it can look overwhelming. But it doesn't have to be.

It's amazing how powerful a learning tool it can be to isolate the rub-pat barrier at the beginning. It establishes a hierarchy of effort for the micromastery. You simply don't have the strength to apply maximum force all the way through. You need the maximum at specific moments only.

Are there any micromasteries that are learned slowly? Certainly some come quicker than others, but if you are having trouble learning a micromastery quickly, it may be because you've missed the effort hotspot—the fast way to conquer the rub-pat barrier at the center of it.

Locate Hidden Micromasteries
(They Are Everywhere)

A micromastery must show a level of skill beyond the ordinary. It must look hard to do and leave people—including yourself—impressed by your achievement. The bigger the challenge, the more learning that is going on. Humans are learning animals, and when we aren't busy learning then we are busy dying, to paraphrase Bob Dylan. As traveler, storyteller, writer, and photographer Tahir Shah puts it: "The only learning curve worth being on is a steep one." When you find yourself on a steep learning curve you simply have to stop messing about and making excuses—it's sink or swim, and humans are good at swimming.

So you look for something hard to do. Let's take gardening as a completely random example—growing a rare tropical plant from seed, grafting one type of orchid onto another to create your own hybrid: these are gardening micromasteries. But you could look further for micromastery ideas, in well-written autobiographical accounts and picture-driven textbooks. *The Education of a Gardener* by Russell Page might be one place to start.* But you have to read it in the right way. Anyone can give the advice "read a textbook," but can you read it with a micromastery hat on? The key is to look for things that are defined and limited in extent, with a verifiable and obvious form of payoff.

In micromastery we are always looking to *make something our own*. Most other learning methods are impersonal, designed for an ideal beginner who doesn't exist in reality. Let's strip our arbitrary choice of gardening down to something really unpromising—lawn care—and see how the micromastery method works.

Lawn care involves cutting the lawn, feeding the grass, getting rid of imperfections by reseeding and rolling the grass. All pretty dull to me except the last one, which conjures up an image of a giant roller I remember from school being used to keep the cricket pitch flat and manned by about six boys all huffing and puffing as they moved it—usually as a punishment for some transgression. I like the idea of this. Okay, I will micromaster rolling the lawn dead flat—maybe for croquet or bowls or a putting green.

Rule 1: Locate the fun

Looking for where the fun is in an activity is the single best way to locate the micromastery that will work for you. It's your way in. Rolling was the only fun image I could conjure up, but I know that if I started researching and asking expert lawn carers I'd find lots more microfun possibilities.

* Russell Page, *The Education of a Gardener* (Collins, 1962; repr. Harvill Press, 2014).

When I returned to analog photography I dutifully tried 35mm film, but it wasn't half as much fun as using a clunky old twin lens camera shooting larger format 120 film. I went where the fun was and devised a micromastery of shooting one film a day, giving me twelve images, which I contact-printed onto a single A4 sheet and stuck in a diary album. I then annotated and drew on the pictures for more fun using a white fiber-tip pen. Repeatable, experimental (I started using all kinds of film, including twenty-year-old Russian film), and with a low rub-pat barrier (balancing exposure and other fiddles against time, which is always short in photography), all of this came from going where the fun was: using a wacky camera and larger-negative film.

I wanted to write fiction and spent a year fiddling about with a novel without making progress and simply getting more anxious. Then a friend suggested I write flash fiction—and not get up from my desk until I'd completed a story. This sounded way more fun than puzzling over a giant, never-ending manuscript. I started writing three a day. It had become a micromastery for fiction writing. Over time I learned the skills I needed to write longer pieces and in the end I did indeed write and publish a full novel.

What we are talking about here is not just the difficulty of getting going with something new—we're talking about specific aspects that somehow chime more deeply with you than others. It's about making it your own. And the key is to listen to your instinctive likes and dislikes when you first approach it.

When I started to get interested in drawing, and began to look at artists' work, I found I instinctively liked the simple technical pen drawings of Dan Price. *That looks fun and I can do that*, I thought—the telltale signs that you've found a way in. It's easy to become dishonest about what you really like and don't like. Advertising bombards us with images that are designed to change our minds, as do movies, TV, shop displays, and the people we meet every day. Sometimes you need to get away and find out what you really like and dislike. A well-meaning artist pal of mine advised me to start drawing with charcoal. But my childhood memories of charcoal were bad. I didn't want to go that way again—I needed something new as my way in. I found I liked the stark black-and-white drawing I had started on my annotated photographs, and that was my way in.

Rule 2: Find the tail and then the dog

The wagging tail is the fun, the way in. But you want to move up to the entire dog—the area you'd like to master or study. In our lawn-care example, rolling leads to a flat lawn, which you want for outdoor games. But there may be patches of less-dense grass—you'll need to reseed these and nurture them. You'll also need to mow the lawn finely, which means getting exactly the right piece of gear—one of those old-style drum mowers rather than a modern rotary. Now that I have my background support in the form of the right gear, and my payoff in having a perfect lawn, and my repeatability in needing to mow it often, I need to break mowing down into the entry trick and experimentation. The entry trick will be found by searching internet sites like YouTube and Instructables, and asking expert lawnmowers of bowling greens what the secrets are. There may be more than one—almost always there is—and these will form the basis of my experimentation. All of which I can integrate with my rolling and planting. Wow—I'm getting really interested! (And interested in a subject I've never even considered before.)

But let's try something completely different. How about international law? I know very little about it and have not much more than a passing interest in it. No doubt if I was personally involved in a case that would be different, but with micromastery we try to find a personal point of contact even if there isn't one initially.

So, go where the fun is. Well, law involves precedents and cases—and these are, essentially, stories. So the way in for me will be about finding the craziest stories that are real cases in international law. I'll naturally want to relate these to others, which is a great way of memorizing them. This can be my entry trick, giving me a big advantage over someone plodding through huge lists on their own. What next?

Rule 3: Go three-dimensional, go multisensory

The latest research into neurological function reveals that much of our brain is composed of multisensory neurons. There isn't one type of brain cell for smell, another separate one for sight—all these inputs can be handled by the same cell. We learn better the more dimensions and senses we involve.

So in the somewhat arid world of international law we need to find more senses and dimensions, which means meeting people, finding real situations—all easily achieved through the internet. Instead of reading, go to an asylum center and see what is going on. Talk to a deep-sea fisherman about where he can and cannot fish—and get some fish from him! Any sensory experiences associated with what we are learning enhance memory and cognition.

Combining fun and three dimensions, I'd want to visit one of the many disputed islands in the world. Get on-the-ground experience by talking to the residents. If I couldn't travel I'd speak on the phone, get them to send pictures. My micromastery might center around attempts to create a new country—Sealand—on an old gas platform in the North Sea, for example. I'd need repeatability, so how about creating a pack of cards featuring disputed islands and territories?

You can see that playing fast and loose with all the various concepts of micromastery helps generate possibilities for future research and inquiry. This is the way you'll find a situation that you can structure using the six-point device of entry trick, rub-pat barrier, background support, the payoff, repeatability, and experimental possibilities.

Rule 4: Talk to the experts

Before bolting the structure of a micromastery onto a new activity you need to talk to people who really know about the subject. An expert, however, isn't quite who you might think. Someone who has done the same job for twenty years has less expertise in my view than a newbie who has found something fun to do. Being able to find fun things to do with a computer program is a more useful form of expertise than knowing the program in some static sense. Children will often be great at finding the fun possibilities in a thing long before they understand it in a formal sense.

Another level of expertise is found in people who are simply able to explain a thing, even though they are not able to do it. You may learn more about writing from an unpublished editor who knows how a story works than, say, a successful novelist who writes intuitively and can't tell you how to write well.

What about drawing again?

I'd been doing Zen circles for a while and started to look around for harder things to draw. I found I liked odd stuff like drawing Italian coffee pots and wicker chairs. Sometimes people were interesting to draw too, but none of these was really a micromastery—they were all too broad. I needed to identify a rub-pat barrier that I could focus on. After more experimentation it dawned on me that primitive art looked a lot like my untutored attempts at drawing, and that the tried-and-tested method of repeating man's own evo-lutionary experience of learning a subject—start math with Euclid, physics with Galileo—was a good idea.

Immediately, I found a rub-pat barrier in flowing lines. All the great artists have lovely lines when they draw. They don't wobble or bend—they flow and arrive at exactly the right spot. Now, this skill is at its most basic in prehistoric art, so by copying examples of it using a rollerball or microfiber-tip pen I could practice, exper-iment and improve at line drawing. I'd found my micromastery.

I have several books of cave art and Paleolithic art and I love the sheer simplicity of the images and the sculptures. I don't claim to understand it—no one really can, as it dates from 10,000 to 30,000 years ago—yet the images remain beautiful and inter-esting. Just as beginner artists find people and faces difficult, so too did their prehistoric counterparts. They mainly didn't bother with faces and instead concentrated on animals—side-on views at that. You can practice endless sweeping curves drawing bison and running horses. You'll also learn some incongruous facts: rhinos were running around France 30,000 years ago engaged in head-butting contests, and our ancestors were drawing pictures of them on cave walls.

From a young age, I had always loved the white horse image cut into the chalk at Uffington in Berkshire—a testament to its power is that it is the symbol of the local district council. This was a typical simplified image using just a few beautiful lines to create the horse shape. By copying this—years later when I started drawing, not when I was younger and simply admiring it—I found it fulfilled the micromastery requirement for experimentation. Varying the lines didn't necessarily spoil the picture—it just created new and weird iterations.

So you see, identifying a micromastery in any area involves something of a survey—but it need not be too detailed. You should learn the activity's hotspots and especially the rub-pat barriers central to it. These may be well known, or you may unearth them by reading interviews with practitioners. And, once you happen on a micromastery, another one—perhaps a better one—may be just round the corner.

Help Yourself

Humans are learning animals—we have to be. Each generation must learn a great deal in order to participate fully in life. Then we must learn what is new and urgent in order to survive the inevitable changes that occur throughout our life. Finally, we must keep learning as we age, in order to keep the basic functionality of our brain in working order.

Since micromastery is an optimal learning strategy as well as an approach to essaying new subjects for potential study, it has many benefits in the life of a learning human.

Your plastic brain: use it or lose it

We are all hostage to the image we have of the way the brain works. For many years it was thought that the amount of gray matter in the brain was fixed—and, worse, that it more or less deteriorated from the age of twenty onward. We now know this to be completely false. Neurological growth and improvement can happen throughout life. Dr. Michael Merzenich, one of the fore-most researchers into brain plasticity, writes:

> Brain plasticity is a physical process. Gray matter can actually shrink or thicken, neural connections can be forged and refined or (conversely) weakened and severed. Changes in the physical brain manifest as changes in our abilities. For example, each time we learn a new dance step, it reflects a change in our physical brains: new "wires" (neural pathways) that give instructions to our bodies on how to perform the step. Each time we forget someone's name, it also reflects brain change—"wires" that once connected to the memory have been degraded, or even severed. As these examples show, changes in the brain can result in improved skills (a new dance step) or a weakening of skills (a forgotten name).*

Never has the phrase "use it or lose it" been better applied than to our plastic brains. Which is where the obvious connections with micromastery begin. Because micromasteries are so diverse, and so fast to learn, we have the opportunity to keep using our brains, to give them the best possible workout, throughout our lives. From an evolutionary perspective a life oriented around micromastery acquisition is far more "natural," i.e. similar to the polymathic lifestyle which our hunter-gatherer forebears experienced, than the curtailed and limited modern experience of mediating life through a computer screen.

---

* Dr. Michael Merzenich, www.onthebrain.com and *Soft-Wired: How the New Science of Brain Plasticity Can Change Your Life* (Parnassus Publishing, 2013).

There is clearly an evolutionary advantage to micromastery, since our brains are wired that way. We unwire them to hyper-specialize at our peril. As we have already mentioned, focal hand dystonia is a debilitating ailment suffered by, among others, classical guitarists. The intense use of one part of the body—the hand and fingers—while the rest remains immobile, rewires the brain to such an extent that it begins to perceive the areas surrounding the fingers and wrist as useless. Over time, this exaggerated difference, following the "use it or lose it" pattern, causes the relatively unused areas to shut down. This results in the loss of control of even the parts needed to play guitar. In the end the guitarist can play nothing. One cure, as we have seen, is to rebuild connections by playing with the whole arm, not just the fingers. This slowly reengages the brain with a balanced (i.e. not over-specialized) neural "picture" of the body.

Hebb's Law ("what fires together, wires together") is a basic observation of neuroscience. If it rains while you take a first trip to Paris, the two will always be connected. But its broader implication is that the greater the variety of experience, the wider the sensory impact, the stronger the trace in the brain, and the greater the connectivity. This not only aids memory but also guards against senility. One wonders at the current epidemic in dementia and must concur with Dr. Merzenich—whose brain-training company treats patients suffering from cognitive decay—that we have made life too lacking in variety and multisensory demand. It is easy to live on autopilot, but do it for too long and basic cognitive abilities fall away. Instead, live polymathically and boost your brain.

Only 3.4 percent of the population are "natural specialists."* The rest of us become that way because of external forces, usually economic. And yet the great "rainmakers" in business are those who invent new products and even new markets by cross-fertilizing ideas from traditionally unconnected zones. By living polymathically they don't just boost their cognitive abilities, they also manage to prosper materially. Use it or lose it.

So long and thanks for the memory

When was the last time you committed something to memory? Now that we have 4G phones we don't need to remember anything, really, yet we're also aware this is a small disaster. Our short- and long-term memories suffer for it.

Merely doing what one has always done, such as a specialist does, strengthens existing networks but builds no new ones in the brain. It also means that short- and medium-term memory are used less and less. The lesson—an intuitive one only recently supported by scientific research—is simple: if you do not use your memory, it will atrophy. If you don't visit new places where you are required to orientate yourself by, for example, learning where the shops are, finding the way back to your hotel, or even remembering where you parked your car, then you'll gradually lose even this basic skill. And it does help to think of memory as a skill.

There are better and worse ways of remembering, and the good

* Rolf Bøe Lindgren, "R. Meredith Belbin's Team Roles Viewed from the Perspective of the Big 5." Research paper, Psychology Institute, University of Oslo, 1997.

news is that there are tricks that work. For example, keeping an accurate journal, perhaps with photographs, improves recall immensely since the major part of memory is *really* looking at what we are trying to recall. When everything is terribly familiar we only glance, look at the outline—and the impression made is weak. As time goes by and familiarity grows we end up living in a world of outlines with no detail at all. For this reason, neuroscientist and learning expert Michael Merzenich always tries to vary his route home, making sure to pay attention to new things he sees each day. He also talks about them, which further helps his memory.

But is this enough? There is something a little ad hoc, and not a little ironic, about using one's memory only when one remembers to. Dr. Stanley Karansky, at ninety years old, described himself as a lifelong self-educator. But rather than dabble, each new interest became an engaging passion, a new subject to master. In an interview with Dr. Norman Doidge he said:

> I became interested in astronomy five years ago and became an amateur astronomer. I bought a telescope because we were living in Arizona at the time and the viewing conditions were so good. . . . I'm willing to put pretty intense concentration and attention into something that interests me at the moment. Then after I feel I've gotten to a higher level at it, I don't pay quite as much attention to that activity and I start sending tentacles to something else.*

* Norman Doidge, *The Brain That Changes Itself: Stories of Personal Triumph from the Frontiers of Brain Science* (Penguin, 2007).

Dr. Karansky was essentially micromastering these various interests before moving on to something new, and this powerful, focused learning paid dividends with his health. Though Dr. Karansky had two heart attacks—one at sixty-five and another at eighty-three—he completely recovered. His parents, who did not share his proclivities for learning, died young—his mother in her forties and his father in his sixties.

Dementia is increasingly associated not just with "not learning," but also with becoming "bored" over time with one's environment and taking less and less acute interest in it. This lack of accuracy degrades working memory, the first stage in many chronic cognitive disorders. The fact that you have permission to learn anything, to experiment and indulge in a skill's gameability once you embrace the micromastery philosophy is a reason never to be bored again.

It's not all about books—utilize your multisensory neurons

Don't think about making art, just get it done. Let everyone else decide if it's good or bad, whether they love it or hate it. While they are deciding, make even more art.

Andy Warhol

Word-based instruction is the way most knowledge is presently passed on. It allows standardization and control. In previous eras a school art lesson was about micromastering drawing. Now, you may also have to read a book about art theory and learn to critique work.

The critical, word-based, book-centered model downplays other ways of learning as inefficient. Simply looking and observing becomes "overlooked." Micromastery, however, is more in tune with the way the brain really works.

The discovery that, rather than having individual, separate senses, the brain is full of multisensory neurons—brain cells that simultaneously record sound, touch, smell, and even pain—has only enhanced the idea of the mind being highly interconnected rather than compartmentalized. We are polymathic by nature. And our senses not only combine with each other but also actually enhance one another. Bacon really does taste better when you can hear it sizzling before you eat it.*

The perception of certain sounds relies on being able to feel those sounds. Research has shown that if you feel a puff of air corresponding to a voiced sound, you recognize that sound better—even if you feel the puff of air on your ankle.†

With so many senses firing close together it is no wonder that synesthesia—the evocation of a sense different from that being directly stimulated—occurs, whereby, for example, people see music as colors.

With the older, erroneous model of the brain, where each sense had its own area, synesthesia was seen as abnormal, a kind of brain damage—not helped by the fact that people with brain damage sometimes exhibited it to a high degree. But with the growing knowledge of multisensory neurons we begin to see that synesthesia, far from being on the periphery of experience, is at its heart.

* Research conducted from 2012 onward by Professor Charles Spence, head of the Crossmodal Research Laboratory at Oxford University's Department of Experimental Psychology.
† Bryan Gick and Donald Derrick (University of British Columbia), "Aero-Tactile Integration in Speech Perception," *Nature* 462 (26 November 2009): 502–4.

Neuroscientists now believe there is a "superstimulus" effect, a sort of mental synergy that can be produced when we combine different senses as we really study something. This embeds deeper connections in the brain, producing faster and better learning and also enabling us to connect to other areas we are interested in.

Micromastery, by seeking out tasks that require us to use more than one sense, realigns us with this better and more natural way of operating.

Are there better and faster ways to learn?

Checking e-mails, sending texts, reading news and blogs—who has time to learn anything, let alone slowly? Though many of us pay lip service to doing slow things like cooking from scratch or travel, we all know how hard it is to hide from a world bent on acceleration. Perhaps the only place to hide is by being deeply immersed in learning something new.

As anyone who has seen a clock's hand slow in a classroom knows, the act of learning actually changes our psychological perception of time passing—making it feel as though time is moving more slowly. But even if it is pleasant to feel one can "slow time down," we still want to make rapid progress in whatever we study.

Michael Merzenich has shown that we learn rapidly when something is novel or startling, or if we are focused intently upon it. In these situations neuron-growth stimulator BDNF* flows and makes stronger, deeper, and better connections. Because each time you practice a micromastery you have to focus intently, it satisfies

* Brain-derived neutrophic factor.

the condition for enhanced learning. Just as importantly, the structure of a micromastery, with its reward and experimental possibilities, makes each attempt novel and interesting, again speeding up learning. And a micromastery is a self-contained watchable unit, which is hugely helpful to rapid learning.

It's so simple but true: we learn fastest by watching others. Aikido levels in the West lagged far behind Japan's until the advent of the internet and the mass sharing of videos and test performances that followed. Now there are aikido practitioners who have never visited Japan but look as if they have trained there. Just watching enables all sorts of subtle connections to be made that mere rules and instruction miss. To restate a crucial point: the hardest part of learning is knowing the relative importance of each bit we learn. When we watch others do it we can glean, from their performance and their demeanor, the relative importance of each element.

Micromastery enhanced by deeper looking

In the Sahara desert I once had a potentially dangerous car problem fixed by a young oasis dweller called Sayed. He wasn't a professional mechanic, but he knew I had a cracked suspension unit just by looking at the stationary car, without actually hearing it or seeing me driving. I didn't believe him until I checked, and only then did I manage to see the slight lean in the car that had alerted him. He told me that all summer as a kid, during the 105–115°F heat of the day, he would crawl under cars to escape the glare. Staring for hours at the exposed undersides of engines had taught him to be a mechanic. "Everything's familiar to me. I know how it connects to everything else," he told me. "By looking hard I learned."

But what does "looking hard" really mean? I suggest a sort of contented wide-angle vision where you aren't trying to solve anything or puzzle anything out. You're waiting for ideas to come to you rather than forcing your own ideas onto what you are observing.

The eighteenth-century German writer and philosopher Johann Wolfgang von Goethe believed that we learned as much from deeply looking at something as we did from the usual scientific method of taking it apart and noting its constituent elements. Goethe saw that by noting the connections between the thing looked at and its environment, its rich context, we gained insights of great value.

I think the key is not to be in a rush. Before visiting a country I often hang its map on the wall. I don't ever really study it, I just kind of live with it, peering at it from time to time. All kinds of ideas for travel and writing about travel have come from this simple activity.

Artists have long considered "deep looking" a way of capturing in the mind's eye the essence of a thing. The writer Bruce Chatwin, who had previously been a director at Sotheby's auction house, believed that having one art object on display which you lived with and slowly consumed with all your senses—eyes, hands, everything—if you could, would, after a while, reveal all its secrets to you. When it was fully digested you sold the piece and obtained another.

By forcing us to accept a limited and contained activity, micromastery facilitates deep looking. Instead of our attention wandering across a vast field we can zoom in and just look, and learn far faster than trying to cram various diverse facts into a protesting brain.

Learning strategies are plastic too

Conventional and outdated wisdom asserts that we each have "learning styles" unique to ourselves. The implication is that if you don't learn using your preferred style you'll fail to acquire the knowledge desired. It also allows you an excuse not to work hard at learning something new. In *Soft-Wired*, however, Michael Merzenich shows that the plasticity of the brain extends to the way we learn. In other words, we can learn how to learn. Indeed, we should focus strongly on doing this.

As well as reading or attending lectures, look at cultivating different learning styles—or, more precisely, learning strategies. As we grow up, the pattern of praise and blame, encouragement and dissuasion builds a bias toward one learning strategy over another. This becomes our default—but it may not be the most effective for you. For example, I convinced myself that I was someone who "learned by doing," so when I got a new camera with an instruction manual an inch thick, I just started using it without more than a glance at where to put the battery. A few months later, I realized that I was hardly scratching the surface of the camera's potential. Reluctantly I sat down to go through the manual, testing things on the camera as I went. For about a week I kept the manual with me, and after pressing buttons and trying things I kept referring back to it. I managed to comprehend everything about operating that camera, and now I relish getting a new manual for something technical. I have found a new learning strategy that has been rewarded, and, thanks to the plasticity of my brain, this strategy is now displacing the previous insistence on always learning by doing.

Micromastery enables you to experiment and use a vast array of different learning strategies. Since all are designed to succeed brilliantly (with a modicum of persistence) at the micromastery concerned, you have a perfect chance to increase your store of potential learning strategies. This in turn increases your *ideational fluency*—your ability to switch between idea sets that may be opposed or contradictory. If one strategy doesn't seem to work, no matter how wedded you are to it, you switch seamlessly to another. Ideational fluency is an attribute required of anyone working in a fast-changing, rapid-learning environment—the kind increasingly encountered today.

Happier and healthier

The vast number of books on happiness reflects our interest in the subject—there are over 500 on Amazon's UK site alone and a whopping 12,000 in the Library of Congress catalog. But how many of them correctly identify happiness as having the curious quality of retreating when you aim too directly at it? You have to sort of sidle up to happiness by doing something else. It catches you best when you're unawares. Sometimes, when we contemplate serious life projects—mountains to scale, careers to prosper at— we lose heart and retreat into consuming rather than doing and producing. Consumption becomes the default source of "happiness," even if we don't want it to be.

Micromastery is one way out. By identifying small, enjoyable and self-contained instances of improvement we move back toward a more real form of happiness.

Happiness is more likely if you make a decision *before* doing an activity: the decision simply to act happy. By acting out the happiness you trust you will find in an area of micromastery, you liberate yourself from the yoke of thinking it is a nebulous "thing" out there, waiting for you to grab hold of it. By deciding to be happy, you shift from a consumer mind-set to a producer mind-set. You focus on the task and not yourself. And when we are in producer mind-set—creating, doing, being active—we tend to be less self-absorbed and become, mysteriously, happier.

And the more dimensions that activity has, the better. Why? Because a multimodal activity—like a micromastery—can combine creativity, learning, enterprise, and physical and intellectual skills. It will stimulate the kind of neurotransmitters and growth factors that will make you feel good about yourself. You'll feel happier, in other words.

Make it happen

John-Paul Flintoff was a successful staff journalist at the *Financial Times*—the world's leading financial newspaper—and he was unhappy. He wasn't sure why. As a youngster he had loved drawing and wanted to be a cartoonist. But this had been discouraged. For years he had earned his living by typing and that was just about all the skilled work his hands did. At the time, there had also been an outbreak of repetitive strain injuries among *FT* journalists, as if the body knew that to do nothing other than type was bad for it. Human beings are polymathic by nature. We have survived as a race by being bricoleurs and DIYers, using our bodies as well as our minds, not as advanced "mind-only" specialists. Flintoff felt that he "wasn't skilled enough" to use his hands for anything except operating a keyboard. "But as a student I'd always had this idea that you were what you did—at that moment," he said. "If you baked bread then you were a baker. I found this idea liberating."

Most of us are trapped by a sense of identity, but we can also derive power from it. By telling others that we are a tree surgeon, an artist, or a sports reporter we feel more empowered to do the job, even if our qualifications are scanty.

Flintoff glimpsed the power of micromastery to outwit the confining straitjacket of identity. When you are making an omelet you're no longer a banker trying to cook—you're someone micromastering a skill.

This was the chink he needed to escape the pressure to conform. He started talking openly about his desire to use his hands after years of only using them to type: "I was at a dinner party talking about this, and someone said that making a shirt was really hard, almost impossible for an amateur. Well, I was worse than an amateur. I was absolutely unskilled. But this was a challenge, which it seems is what I needed."

Flintoff went home and started out on an unplanned micromastery—he was going to make a shirt from scratch. He found an old one, unpicked its seams and laid out the parts. Just doing this was very instructive. He then used these parts as templates to cut from new cloth. He managed to construct a brand-new shirt that looked pretty good. Now that he had the basic model, he could experiment with it. He tried swapping parts out, oversizing certain sections of the shirt, messing with collars and lengths. He had his own experimental test bed right there in the form of his sewing machine and his newly developed skills. But he didn't stop there—he went on to make all sorts of other garments, including jackets and trousers.

Flintoff could have approached learning to be a tailor rather differently. He could have mastered the basics of sewing—tacking, using the machine for various stitches, practicing doing button-holes on a blank piece of cloth, sewing rags together—and it's likely that he would have given up, with what he had learned drib-bling away to nothing.

How many of us learned math, French, geography, chemistry at school and, having never used what we learned, now recall almost nothing? When you learn the basics it never sticks, unless you keep going to achieve something permanent like a micromastery—a dis-tinct and recognizable unit of skill. Since most people never get past the basics except in their specialism, most people lose most of what they learn. All of which would be supremely depressing if we didn't naturally accumulate micromasteries, even if the formal aca-demic culture is against them or refuses to take them seriously.

Flintoff set aside his conventional education—and he has a lot of it, including a master's degree in English. He hadn't lost faith in the academic method—he simply returned to what we do as children. We look for something we like and try to copy it.

Flintoff told me he became "incredibly happy" using his hands again to make something other people admired and thought difficult to do. He had discovered the immense rewards that micro-mastery can bring. He was so liberated by his shirt making that he went on to write a book about it called *Sew Your Own* (Profile

Books, 2010). He also found that his fear of learning new things had deserted him. He went on to study improvisational acting under the theater genius (a term I use sparingly) Keith Johnstone. He became a life coach. He started singing and he returned to his childhood love of drawing comics. Micromastery can be a small thing, a simple thing—but it can lead you into previously unimagined realms of happiness.

Produce or consume

The "specialist-centric" model of human existence is an economic model. If you are a specialist—say, making shoes all day—then society benefits and you benefit. You no longer have to milk the cow and sow corn and go fishing. But what if you *like* doing those things? What if making shoes is OK when you do it three days a week, but it drives you insane if you have to do it twelve hours a day, five days a week in an open-plan office after a two-hour commute?

Producing is more satisfying than consuming. Consuming is what is eating up the planet's resources and polluting the sea. Of course, a nice meal is enjoyable—there is no need to scarf down cans of baked beans and suffer. But micromastery switches us to a more productive view of life. We come to see that making things is simply *better*.

Happiness comes from inside—it's a decision. Enjoyment comes from outside—it has to be sniffed out. Enjoyment gets you out of bed in the morning, but happiness helps you sleep at night. In general, the enjoyment derived from production is far more durable than the enjoyment we get from consuming.

Boost confidence

Micromasteries build confidence step by step. The more micro-masteries you have under your belt, the more confident as a person you will be. And not just because of the skills you gain specific to each micromastery. You will develop skills that are transferable between micromasteries—rapid learning, structural information about knowledge acquisition, performance skills, memory improvement—which is an empowering thing.

Confidence plays a hugely important part in learning. But what is it? My younger self imagined confidence as some kind of inner feeling of supremacy where nothing could make me scared or nervous. But I discovered that many seemingly superconfident people are plagued by all kinds of self-doubt. Sometimes the appearance of confidence—fast-talking, loud, and humorous behavior—masks the very opposite feelings.

The sci-fi writer A. E. van Vogt put it best when he said that confidence is simply the ability to say your name clearly and loudly enough when asked, to greet someone warmly and to congratulate them if they have something to be congratulated for. Nothing else. In other words, forget the inner feelings and make a performance decision instead. To the external observer, there is no difference between the man who can talk to anyone at the bus stop and the person who tells himself, against an inner timidity, to do so and succeeds. You see this kind of process in its most extreme form when a former stammerer goes on to become a gifted public speaker.

So confidence is really a performance decision to put more energy into what you do. More directed effort is like very deliberately opening a tap, allowing energy to pour out instead of hoping it will find its way out magically. If we lack confidence, we might assume the meager energy at our disposal is all we have. But all we need to do is make that performance decision, turn the tap, and give it more effort. When learning to sing, lack of confidence causes the singer to put less energy into the voice, which results in it going more easily out of tune (off-balance). This, in turn, further weakens confidence. To break the downward cycle all you have to do is put *more* energy into your singing when you feel yourself going out of tune, not less. It's a case of consciously opening the tap rather than waiting for inspiration.

Lack of confidence often means we just don't try, and the single biggest cause of failure is not trying. When people self-describe as "failing" or being a "failure," it usually transpires that they merely entertained a notion but did nothing further about it. They didn't take the extra step. They believed that "it wasn't worth it" or "too many others are already doing it" or "I'm not good enough." But you are.

Micromastery as confidence ladder

In all areas, rung by rung, we ascend a ladder of increasing confidence. With a micromastery, by its very nature, you gain full confidence before you move on to something more demanding. This is made possible by:

Easy experimentation through repeatability. A micromastery is small and fast, easily repeatable. Repeatability breeds confidence. And if you can experiment each time you repeat, you can gain extra confidence. You'll be extending your range. The steepened learning curve will still be within your mental limits.

Beating one-off paranoia. "It was a fluke," "beginner's luck"—how many times have you heard these kinds of expressions in response to honest encouragement of early potential? Of course, beginner's luck exists—the firmament looks kindly on bold learners—but that isn't a reason to be paranoid about early success. Take everything you have going for you and use it to fuel your improvement. The accusation of beginner's luck is reduced by the fact that repeatability is built into each micromastery. It is not designed to be a one-off—so how can it be subject to one-off luck?

Because a micromastery is a small and repeatable thing it can very easily be demonstrated that you are improving. Many people have gone years without learning anything new, which has severely atrophied their confidence and ability to learn. With a micromastery you can beat this vicious circle by watching visible external signs of incremental progress.

Acknowledging that show-offability is a social requirement. Some people might deride or belittle the human need for attention, but we all need it—some more than others—and we all learn how to get it—some of us better than others. Now, if you aren't getting enough of the right kind of attention why not get more with your micromastery, and use this "attention payment" as a reward to keep going? The committed and virtuous may shun such a reward, but I know that when you are on a steep learning curve you need all the help you can get.

However, there is another factor at work. Lack of confidence is connected to not liking to be watched or on display. People who lack confidence can feel a reluctance even to say their own names loudly in public and they rather dread those little intro speeches you have to do at seminars and courses. (I should know, because that's me as well.)

It isn't the *watching* so much as the *imagined judging* that is the problem. You may be quite happy to try your three-card trick in front of a couple of friendly eight-year-olds—but not a snarky teenager. No one likes to be judged, but a micromastery puts you outside the judging zone because it is only one of many versions. Doing the task badly matters less. When I make an omelet for someone I could get nervous—what if I fail? But then I remember that the whole point is that I am on the path to mastery, not one-off success. This is just one more step, and if they say it is less than perfect I'll try hard to thank them sincerely for deigning to eat my food. And my next one will be better.

Refine and reboot your bucket list

Though I prefer the more positive-sounding term "wish list," I have a strong belief in such lists as a life-changing tool. We can either look at life as something externally driven—getting promoted, elected, chosen, cheered—or we can choose to look at it as something we have more control over: a simple list of things we wish to have done before we are too frail to do anything.

Micromasteries in some form or another feature high on most people's wish lists. American author and polymath Clifford A.

Pickover—a great proponent of the wish list—has several in his top ten:*

1. Play Bach's Toccata and Fugue in D Minor
2. Learn Ch'ang-style Tai Chi
3. Obtain a PhD
4. Write a novel and sell it
5. Raise Amazon Golden Severum fish
6. Play bass guitar in a rock band
7. Eat spicy tekka maki
8. Own a Mitsubishi 3000GT sports car with stick shift
9. Fire an Uzi and a .45 Magnum
10. Publish a technical paper with a triple integral symbol

Though firing an Uzi machine gun is hardly a micromastery, doing it well is. And while owning a sports car with a manual gearbox might seem a little devoid of skill, driving it in the manner it deserves is also susceptible to micromastery.

Pickover is a likeably eccentric polymath who has written over thirty books that range from science fiction to hard math. He has many patents to his name and is a specialist in speech-recognition software research, which he pursues in his day job as a fellow at the Thomas J. Watson Research Center in New York. As you might guess from his list (most of which he has achieved), he has micro-mastered a wide range of skills. Google his "wishing project" for more on this.

* Clifford Pickover, *Sex, Drugs, Einstein, and Elves* (Smart Publications, 2005).

The whole of Pickover's ethos is polymathic in nature: use cross-fertilization from different fields to advance both your life and your specialist area (if you have one).

The problem with the wish list is that it can become a list of consumables rather than real achievements. And it is a little weird to do things solely to "look back on them." Surely they should be good at the time too? There needs to be balance. By making a wish list of micromasteries you have something that is interesting to do, useful forever, *and* nice to look back on.

Micromastery and a flow state of mind

Flow is a concept we touched upon at the start of the book, popularized by the Czech psychologist Mihaly Csikszentmihalyi. The central idea is that when we become fully immersed in activity we enter a state of mind where we're no longer conscious of time. Concentration is enhanced and we feel fully alive, though reflecting on such things can interrupt the flow state. It is only in retrospect that we recall such feelings. When you are in a flow state, your critical stop/go judging way of thinking is switched off. You learn faster as a result.

While conventional ways of learning actually militate against achieving it, micromastery encourages the formation and sustaining of a flow state. Take the simple act of drawing Zen circles, which we looked at in "What is Micromastery." You can easily drop into the semi-meditative and fully immersed flow state while endlessly attempting to draw the perfect calligraphic circle with pen or brush. You can easily achieve what might even be called a micro flow state when you dip in and practice for ten or fifteen minutes a language or a skill that is relatively simple, such as spinning a basketball on your finger.

Getting into a flow state of mind is something that improves with practice. You begin by identifying a challenge that you have the skills to master. If the challenge is greater than the skills you need, you'll notice that your arousal levels rise (even causing anxiety if your skills are poor). If your skills are over and above what the challenge requires, you enter what is called a "control" state—which over time can degenerate into boredom. In between being agitated and being too much in control lies the flow state. Start by really focusing, 100 percent, because distractions are fatal. Set aside enough time (although a flow state is timeless, time pressure will stop it happening). Finally, monitor your own inner state: Are you anxious, bored, energized?

A micromastery is almost a perfect method to experience flow—the challenge is precise, the skills needed are not hard to learn. When you enter the repetition and experimentation stage of micromastery you can improve awareness of flow by monitoring yourself on the spectrum from boredom through to arousal/anxiety. Use numbers: 0 for bored, 1 for relaxed, 2 for control, 3 for flow, 4 for arousal, 5 for anxious. Up the challenge if it feels routine. If you find you are getting nervy and agitated, slow down, lower the challenge, and then work on your skills. Hitting the "3" sweet spot is amazing. Time stands still. I have practiced micromastering line sketches and thought it was lunchtime when it was 4:30 p.m.—four hours just disappeared in a state of full concentration and enjoyment. It was a complete sense of "being present."

Escape the "overcomplicated" trap

Complexity scientist Samuel Arbesman's book *Overcomplicated* relates a common problem in this world: we are losing control of it through the sheer proliferation of systems and technologies that govern our lives (and which we don't fully understand).*

Micromastery provides, in miniature, an opportunity for simplicity and subtlety. One can experiment with omelet-making and learn all its inner secrets without being trapped by overcomplication. With each new level of subtlety, the brain assigns single neurons to do the task that earlier on in learning required a whole ring of neurons.

The world is an incredible place but in the last hundred years it has become a very complicated one in which to live. Most of human existence has been spent as hunter-gatherers—a simple life but one which has all sorts of possibilities for mastery. It's an existence where you can start small and humble at anything. But, though we have created many wonderful toys and improvements, we've also created a "complication threshold" over which anyone interested must pass. And it simply puts people off. You can't just do stuff—you need the right tools, qualifications—maybe a doctorate, insurance, permission . . . We're put off by how everything seems to be so darned complicated, and the reaction is either rejection or to give in and embrace some tiny corner of complicated

---

* Samuel Arbesman, *Overcomplicated: Technology at the Limits of Comprehension* (Penguin, 2016).

ritual. (I have a friend who revels in oil company contracts, sees them as promising a sort of near enlightenment after the workout they've given his brain.) Or you can throw away everything that smacks of complexity—which includes the subtle—but then the world becomes dumb and stupid.

We need to avoid drowning in complexity. By breaking tasks down into micromasteries we return to a world in which simplicity and subtlety can retain a useful place.

Multiple Micromastery and Synergy

Having one micromastery is nice, but the nature of the game is to want more. If your micromasteries are all in the same field—whether that be craft beer making, tap dancing, or nuclear physics—then you are closing in on mastery. It makes sense to define a master as someone who is supercompetent at a required number of micromasteries within his or her field.

Serious learning requires that we stay focused and on track, but this doesn't mean we have to be interested in only one thing for all of our lives. It's important not to confuse the correct learning strategies—which very definitely require you to be focused and on track—with living strategies, which have more subtle requirements. Doing the same thing every day of your life will kill you with boredom; doing the same thing every day for a period of time while you aim to master something is a proven and effective learning strategy. You then switch to something new, maybe a new micromastery. Be on track until you find yourself in a rut, then switch tracks.

Micromastery makes switching tracks pain-free, easy, and part of the program. We aren't meant to be specialists. As we mentioned earlier, one study showed that only 3.4 percent of the population are naturally inclined to specialization. If you are part of the rest of the population, read on, and even if you aren't, read on. According to extensive research for UNESCO by Dr. Robert Root-Bernstein:

> We found that compared with typical scientists, Nobel laureates are at least 2 times more likely to be photographers; 4 times more likely to be musicians; 17 times more likely to be artists, 15 times more likely to be craftsmen; 25 times more likely to be writers of non-professional writing, such as poetry or fiction and 22 times more likely to be performers, such as actors, dancers or magicians.*

These Nobel Prize–winning scientists are specialists, but they enhance their specialty with outside interests, thus gaining new perspectives.

Being polymathic isn't just the province of the genius; it's open to everyone. All you need are multiple micromasteries. The current interest in the portfolio career reflects our need, and willingness, NOT to stick to one occupation all the time. And as we've seen, even if you do desire a more conventional single-occupation career, it pays to feed it with multiple micromasteries.

Suppose you have a child who seems unusually talented at

* R. Root-Bernstein and M. Root-Bernstein, "Keynote Speech: Arts at the Center," paper presented at UNESCO The Second World Conference on Arts Education, Seoul, Korea, 25–28 May 2010: 7-8; www.unesco.org/culture/en/artseducation/pdf/fullpresentationrootbernstein.

science and appears to have a natural inclination toward math and physics. You might be tempted to engage a math tutor, hopeful that your offspring will achieve great things thanks to early specialization. Walter Alvarez, a doctor, saw things differently. His son Luis was gifted in science, but he chose to balance this by sending him to a school noted for arts and crafts. Instead of fasttracking through advanced calculus, Luis worked at technical drawing and woodwork, which didn't stop him from going on to study science later and ultimately win the 1968 Nobel Prize in Physics. Luis attributed his success to his ability to build any experimental apparatus he could imagine.

Developing fine motor skills was also essential to the success claimed by celebrated U.S. astronaut Story Musgrave. He grew up on a farm, where he learned the skills "to fix anything," which was just as crucial in a space station as it was to his later degrees in engineering and medicine.

There is informal recognition of the advantage of a polymathic background: 82 percent of scientists and engineers surveyed by Robert Root-Bernstein answered "Yes" to the question "Would you recommend an arts-and-crafts education as a useful or even essential background for a scientific innovator?"* Arts and crafts are the natural home of micromastery—self-contained, scalable, repeatable, defined.

Scientists and engineers are not alone in needing inspiration from elsewhere. Artists and writers also gain from having a

* Robert Root-Bernstein et al., "Entrepreneurship in Science and Engineering Correlates with Sustained Arts and Crafts Participation," Invited lecture, National Endowment for the Arts and the Brookings Institution, Washington, DC, 10 May 2012.

non-arts background. W. H. Auden, Somerset Maugham, Anton Chekhov, and David Foster Wallace all had math or science educations in addition to their literary pursuits. Foster Wallace was also a junior tennis player. Jack Kerouac and Ken Kesey were both American football players; Albert Camus played in goal for the Algerian national soccer team; and Samuel Beckett was a notable cricket player in his native Ireland (the only Nobel laureate to feature in the *Wisden Cricketers' Almanac*).

When he was a child, Alexis Carrel, Nobel Prize winner in Medicine in 1912, was taught by his lace-making mother how to stitch incredibly tiny and intricate patterns. He later used this skill in making ground-breaking advancements in the field of surgery.

Hans von Euler-Chelpin focused on fine arts at college before an interest in color led him to the sciences, and he would eventually win the 1929 Nobel Prize in Chemistry. Leading astrophysicist Jacob Shaham claimed, "Acting taught me how to read equations like a script with characters I had to bring to life."

All these high achievers demonstrate the same thing: there is great synergy in having multiple areas of expertise. Synergy means, among other things, that the whole is greater than the sum of its parts. By having several micromasteries you are not just a great person who has some impressive life hacks to show off; each one of those micromasteries enhances the acquisition of more knowledge, so that you can deploy it with greater effect.

Synergy between different areas of knowledge (not just academic but also practical) is little studied. After all, what field would it come under? One of the few to have studied it is Carl Gombrich of University College London. He has found that students who study sciences *and* arts at A Level (a minority in the

UK) are later more likely to have positions of responsibility and leadership—by six orders of standard deviation, a hugely positive correlation.* The more you know, and the greater number of different perspectives you have on things, the exponentially better it is for you. Fields of knowledge cross-fertilize in many, often surprising, ways. The kernel of creativity is, after all, putting together things that have never been put together before.

Synergy is the extra energy liberated in a system when its constituent parts benefit each other. In a sense it's like an economy of scale for a system. It's not a new idea—in fact it's been around since Aristotle. The usual one-line definition is that "the whole is greater than the sum of the parts" but that tends to deflate the truly mysterious nature of synergy.

As well as systems synergy there are synergies in creativity—the cross-fertilizing of previously unrelated ideas to make new ones. We have seen how skills can sabotage each other at the rub-pat barrier, but there are also synergetic skills. For example, competence in aikido will help any kind of bodily skill acquisition, from golf to dancing.

Systems thinking involves looking at a system in its entirety rather than breaking it down into bits. A stationary car is merely a collection of parts, but a car+driver is a system. If you want, say, to win a Formula 1 race you think of the entire system of control and feedback involving the driver and the car he is driving. If you

---

* Carl Gombrich, "Polymathy, New Generalism, and the Future of Work: A Little Theory and Some Practice from UCL's Arts and Sciences Degree," in William C. Kirby and Marijk van der Wende (eds.), *Experiences in Liberal Arts and Science Education from America, Europe, and Asia: A Dialog Across Continents* (Palgrave Macmillan, 2016), pp. 75–89.

think solely in a reductionist way, looking at engine, gearbox, aerodynamics, you'll end up with a less than optimal solution. With the car+driver system we can come up with synergetic combinations that take into account the driver's relationships with different parts of the car. We can optimize these relationships and the driver's skills with tire and fuel combinations that particularly suit him.

In a way systems thinking is with us in everyday life when we consider the effect of an institution, say a school, on an individual. We informally acknowledge the synergy of a "good school," the subtle combination of ethos, resources, and good teachers that a skilled principal knows how to marshal.

Anyone who has done group exercise has probably experienced the synergy when the whole group tries hard and each individual gets a boost in stamina that they would never get if training alone.

(These examples also perhaps indicate how slippery a concept synergy can be, and why reductionists are suspicious of it. This is summed up in the joke about the reductionist scientist who tears a butterfly apart, labels each part, and when asked where the butterfly has gone answers, "What butterfly?")

Synergy is experienced as a sudden addition of energy—a quantum leap—rather than a linear progression, a steady rise. When you already have several micromasteries they can all improve suddenly when you learn another one.

People hoping to master martial arts often report flat progress. They are on the plateau. Then suddenly they go up a level, make a quantum leap. It can be so exciting, and they expect the rise to continue, but soon they level out to a new plateau. That quantum rise is the synergy between the micromasteries.

You can break a big area of activity into smaller micromasteries. It's the usual way to learn everything from cooking to martial arts. Aikido, for example, requires learning several micromasteries: four different locks, various takedowns and throws, precise methods of stepping and moving. As you acquire each micromastery in turn it helps a little with the ones you already know. Some are particularly synergetic—they naturally boost each other. When attempting to master an entire field it makes sense to map it out with progressive and synergetic micromasteries. This is different from "mastering the basics." Each micromastery stands alone and does not need the others in order to make sense. However, its acquisition informs existing micromasteries and helps all-around improvement.

Skills transfer

The more you know, the easier it gets—not just in foreign languages and sports but in every area of learning. There is a crossover in skills and perspectives and insights. Sometimes these areas of crossover can be quite close—pilots who are used to one type of plane are retrained quickly for another type by maximizing the common knowledge needed for both—but much wider skill transfer is possible. Yukio Mishima, the Japanese novelist, was a fourth dan black belt at kendo and a first dan at karate. Though he was a late starter at both sports and stiff in his movements, his tests were described as very impressive. Mishima said that when he was being tested for his black belt he just switched into the same frame of mind he used when writing.

Writers such as D. H. Lawrence, Henry Miller, and Jean Cocteau were also well-regarded visual artists—the kind of sensibilities formed by their writing gave their art power and conviction, even though they were not trained in drawing and painting.

Crossover skills can include timing and intensity of action. From aikido I learned how to apply maximum force with little preparatory movement or thought. I have found this experience of delivering full-on power in bursts useful when mastering new skills as diverse as kneading bread or using a bow drill to make fire.

Shift your perspective

How fast can you shift perspective? In a changing world with evolving technologies it is no longer a luxury. Having identified some of your own micromasteries, your identity undergoes a subtle shift. Instead of a "one-size-fits-all" perspective conditioned by your work identity you can try on another suggested by a micromastery. You get used to changing your perspective. You could, for example, ask of any problem how a canoeist or a chef, for example, might look at it.

By adopting the polymathic perspective, one of ideational fluency, gained from having multiple micromasteries, you automatically switch from "closed" to "open." By this I mean a general view on life, a feeling of being open to life's wonders, marvels, and opportunities. You become open to learning. Because you know the micromastery secret of acquiring expertise, you don't feel shut out by the expertise of others. You become quietly confident and fearless, a good combination in any circumstance.

Being stuck, rigid, unable to move is what stops progress. Sometimes we throw money at the problem or use excessive force, half knowing that we're going to break the thing before we start. We go head on and often meet massive opposition to what we're trying to achieve. Military strategies that emphasize a straight charge usually fail; a feint and a surprising flank attack work much better. This is what changing your viewpoint does for you. But you can only change viewpoints if you have another. And as a polymathic micromaster, of course, you will.

The mysteries of mastery

In this book about micromastery, mastery itself remains forever on the horizon. Micromastery has many elements in common with mastery, but it is also often simply the first step toward it. Let's look a little closer at what we mean by mastery itself.

Being a master of something—what an enviable thing! We imagine the master has a more satisfying life, deeper insights into reality. We know that masters must spend long hours honing their skill. There is usually some kind of apprenticeship. The main thing is the amount of time—10,000 hours according to recent popular research—though it's easy to be a little skeptical about that, as time alone is not enough. The manner of the master is all important—his or her attitude to learning and improving their skill.

Mastery is about keeping going, mainly. It is about being comfortable on the plateau. It's about the long haul, not the quick fix or the shortcut. Shortcuts are attractive but they are never easy. Usually they involve greater energy and commitment, which can result in burnout. When I watched aikido masters in Japan I saw how they enjoyed their training; they didn't try too hard because they knew they were in it for the long haul. The mantra of the master is "whatever keeps you on the path to mastery is good, whatever causes you to deviate is bad."

Mastery is about seeing the deep relationships and important causative features. When I started aikido I thought it was all about getting the right angle, the right move. Slowly I realized that it was more important to think about stance and balance. When these are right you do the right moves almost automatically.

Mastery requires commitment—but of the right kind. You can't be too keen or too obsessed, otherwise you won't see the wood for the trees. On the other hand you have to do a lot of it. As master photographer Daidō Moriyama always says, you just have to take a lot of pictures.

Balance is built into every layer of what we call mastery—the fine and ever finer balance between doing too much and not enough. And balance is one of those things you have to feel—at first, maybe, in the diluted form you may find in a book or instructional video. But then you'll have to learn to feel it yourself. One reason Japanese master carpenters do so much work by eye is to build up an enhanced trust in their intuitive powers of seeing and appreciating good balance.

Masters keep going at what they do. They bend before opposition but do not break; they take the path of least resistance, as long as it still is the path. Masters use ritual instead of repetition to achieve long-term, maybe even dimly conceived, goals. Ritual is making repetition into something fun that you look forward to, or at least tolerate. You can make a ritual out of anything—even checking e-mails. You have your special e-mail-checking chair, a cup of Ethiopian coffee best drunk at 116°F, your e-mail-checking hat . . . you get the picture.

George Leonard, a master of aikido and also of writing about mastery, noted that there comes a point when you have to surrender to your craft or field. You have to take it on its own terms. This makes you open and noncritical at a time when criticism is of little use. It means you stop talking and start watching. It is the point when mild obsession can take over.

You cannot become mechanical, though, which is where obsession will ultimately take you. You need to maintain that experimental drive—testing, looking, observing. You need to take risks from time to time, knowing full well that some will fail with a resounding fanfare. And some will always be an astonishing success . . .

Polymathic Paradise

We are taught that focusing on and specializing in one thing alone is the key to success and happiness in life. The latest versions of this credo usually include constant references to "passion." However, you'll discover that the opposite is in fact true. Oh, sure, at the moment of engagement all successful people are 100 percent focused—but that is only for a small fraction of their lives. The rest of the time they either rest or draw nourishment from elsewhere. We've already seen that Nobel Prize-winning scientists— the very definition of a single-minded specialist—are actually many times more likely to study arts, crafts, or music than an ordinary academic scientist. But they keep it quiet. In a specialist culture the polymathic impulse has to be hidden.

A polymath uses their multiple areas of expertise and interest to feed and nurture their specialism (if they are a specialist), providing new perspectives and energy. Polymathic people have higher energy and more interest in life, and are happier and less fragile. They are OPEN rather than closed—the default setting of those following a singular path.

Until this very recent historical period people had to be poly-mathic just to survive. But the proliferation of complex industrial manufacturing techniques, huge economies of scale in all areas of food production, the ubiquity of mass entertainment through TV and the internet, and the computerization of even the lowest-level work have enabled the specialist worldview to proliferate—at the expense of our very human polymathic selves.

Entrepreneurial, innovative, and creative activity all require a polymathic outlook. At the highest levels of science, polymathy is alive and well—scientists constantly borrow from other fields to make progress in their own. The key problem now is simply how to reintroduce our lost heritage of multiple expertise into every-day lives and jobs.

After university, instead of following a traditional career path I went to Japan and spent three years learning martial arts. While there I glimpsed the idea that, over time, would become micromas-tery. One whole year was spent in a traditional dojo shared with the Tokyo Riot Police. I went from zero to black-belt instructor level by virtue of studying five hours a day, five days a week, but this was almost incidental: the real benefit was in discovering how to learn.

The Japanese way of teaching is to break everything down into self-sustaining routines which work on their own but also lead into the greater whole. Part of this is kata—repetitive movements such as punching and kicking—but part of it in aikido becomes "tech-niques"—self-contained ways of immobilizing an opponent. Within a single technique such as the shoulder takedown *shihon nage* there are endless variations—different ingredients and cooking times, if you like—which enable experimentation and growth in the student. One very able practitioner of aikido only ever studied this one technique—and the discipline's founder, Morihei Ueshiba, famously wrote that "the whole of aikido was in *shihon nage*."

Over the next few years I refined the ideas I had picked up in Japan. I found *Learning How to Learn* by Idries Shah (Octagon Press, 1978) a particularly useful book in further developing the wider notions and implications of polymathy. Already I saw that overspecializing in one subject was something of an illusory path.

Viktor Frankl, in his 1946 classic of survival in the concentration camps of Germany, *Man's Search for Meaning* (new edition, Rider, 2004), proved, as much as it is possible to do so, that man is not a pain-avoiding, pleasure-seeking android—rather he or she is primarily driven by meaning. He identified three areas which increase meaning in everyday life: caring for others; artistic, creative, or productive endeavors; and choosing one's own attitude to suffering and misfortune.

The idea that life is about specializing leads to a diminution of meaning. The narrower your worldview, the more everything outside it looks meaningless. Only your narrow sliver of activity holds any value for you. You find you care less for other activities and the people who do those things. The less you create, make, and produce, the less meaningful the world will seem.

If you suffer pain or loss, as we all must in our lives, mental flexibility—ideational fluency—in reframing and reconfiguring our situation can often mean the difference between life and death. The intimate connection between healthy mental and physical states is constantly being affirmed by new generations of researchers. A polymathic state of mind simply has more resources for dealing with life's blows than the singular, specialist mentality.

Going for a Burton

I studied the lives of over a hundred famous geniuses and poly-maths. Two of them—Richard Francis Burton, the Victorian ex-plorer, and Claude Shannon, the father of information theory—hold particular fascination for me.

Burton could supposedly read and write in over twenty lan-guages, and yet he had been sacked from university after just a year in which he spent most of his time bunking off with gypsies or other slack undergraduates (the exact offense that did for him was to drive a coach and horses through town on a day proscribed for such behavior).

He was an indifferent university student but he changed when he joined the Indian Army—where he specialized in languages—studying for up to eleven hours a day but always in bursts of fifteen minutes, switching between areas within the same subject. It is common among polymaths to see such periods of intense and specialized interest as a key to learning. It is a kind of "serial obsession" very different from multitasking—which has been shown to be less efficient.

Burton took leave of the army and began exploring in the Mid-dle East, where he entered Mecca in disguise, and Africa, where his account *The Lake Regions of Central Africa* became a kind of guidebook for future explorers, including Livingstone and Stanley.

Burton had many interests, many of which—exploration, trans-lating, fencing—he performed at the highest level (he was judged to be one of Britain's finest swordsmen). He had, like Goethe and

Leonardo before him, cracked one of the secrets of polymathy—mastery, up to a point, is transferable.

Juggling genius

Claude Shannon is the father of information theory, a veritable genius of early computer development who contributed to many areas of science. His master's thesis—"A Symbolic Analysis of Relay and Switching Circuits"—has been called by mathematician Howard Gardner "possibly the most important and most famous master's thesis of the century." He then switched from electrical engineering to biology to write a PhD thesis on "An Algebra for Theoretical Genetics."

The polymathic Shannon was also a keen juggler, unicyclist, and chess player. He wrote the first chess-playing computer program and invented many things, both useful and humorous, including a motorized pogo stick and a rocket-powered flying disc.

It was Shannon's interest in the micromastery of juggling that led to some very fruitful ideas and also demonstrated that something apparently useless—juggling is mere entertainment to many—is actually a fascinating "gateway skill"—one that leads you from the tail to the body of the dog.

The earliest depiction of juggling (and wrestling) is found in the comic-like figures on a wall in the Beni Hasan tombs in Upper Egypt overlooking the banks of the Nile near El Minya. These pictures date from 1994 to 1781 B.C.—nearly 4,000 years ago. Other cultures such as the ancient Chinese, South American, and Indian all practiced juggling through the ages. In Europe it became a staple of fairs and traveling shows, often synonymous with jesting and trickery.

Shannon was intrigued by juggling partly because he found it difficult—he had small hands—but also because it provided a great insight into lots of problems involved in robotics. He went on to make the world's first bounce juggling machine (bounce juggling is when you drop the ball and catch it after it bounces, rather than throw it upward). He showed that if a machine can be taught to juggle—or designed to juggle—then it should be easy to make it into an efficient construction-line robot.

Shannon was also fascinated by unicycles—he often rode one along the corridors of the Massachusetts Institute of Technology. Riding the unicycle is, again, a classic instance of a micromastery. Shannon had latched on to something humans find hard—and therefore fruitful for study. He took his interest a step further by making a robot unicycle. For this he needed to invent balance systems far in advance of what was available, and his discoveries were able to benefit all kinds of robot manufacture. Here a micromastery provided a distinct problem in a playful guise that could be solved for the benefit of all. I think that Shannon stumbled on an approach that scientists might well be able to use as a creative research tool.

It was certainly used by another genius—Richard Feynman. Bored with physics after his PhD, he sat in the university cafeteria and idly watched someone spinning a plate on their finger (spinning anything on the fingers is a classic micromastery). He watched the decorative design on the plate undergo a strange wobble and wondered if he could describe it mathematically. Suddenly he was engaged—he was playing with math because the situation wasn't serious. (Feynman would later say that he made a decision then to have ONLY a playful attitude to problems.)

Shannon, too, was famous for his playful approach and his crazy inventions (including the "ultimate machine," where a box, when switched on, opened, a hand appeared and then switched off the machine before folding back into the box). Micromastery is essentially a playful activity; that's one of its great strengths. When Feynman finished playing with the math of the plate he found that it could actually be used to describe some knotty problems in subatomic physics. He opened up the whole field of quantum electrodynamics and went on to win a Nobel Prize.

Creativity Explosion

Simply growing up in the premodern period guaranteed a certain polymathic background. Making and repairing skills were not only common but also necessary for ordinary life. Having fun involved work and thought rather than deft handling of a remote control. The ease and comfort provided by modern transport, communications, and entertainment have stripped away this polymathic grounding—a world in which a butcher, a banker, or a miner's wife could also be a wonderful violinist and expert watercolorist. Even if such statements veer toward the sentimental and ideal, they can be an inspiration for those wanting to reclaim the potential promised by micromastery.

I've always found it weird that it is only as we surge toward greater specialization and mechanization that we begin to talk about creativity and innovation. The great inventors of the past had no need to talk of brainstorming or lateral thinking. They did it naturally. People like Thomas Edison and Alexander Graham Bell didn't need lessons in creative thinking because they already had such a diverse range of information and skills ready to deploy.

It is interesting that the rise in creative thinking as a subject exactly parallels the disappearance of what gives rise to it: diversity of knowledge, information, and perspective.

Micromastery and boosted creativity

Isn't the world crying out for more science graduates? More numerate specialists? Michael Brooks, curator of the Waterloo Global Science Initiative Learning 2013 summit in Ontario, points out that theoretical physicists, technology managers, and even the CEO of Lockheed Martin agree that more science graduates are not the answer. While it is true that low-level positions can be filled by numerate graduates—there is not a problem here and wages haven't risen in this area for good reason—the problem is higher up. The conventional specialized science graduate seems to lack organizational, communication, and management skills. So a gap opens up where the real creative work needs to be done. Brooks suggests a big change is required in the way people are recruited into university. They need smart, creative people with multiple micromasteries.

Seeing resemblances and generalizing, learning from one thing and recognizing something a bit similar—this is how our mind navigates the world. The wider our base of knowledge the greater our source of patterns and examples. How do we create new ideas? By cross-fertilizing old ones. Again, the wider our potential base of new ideas, the greater their variety and the more powerful our creativity.

If you know about chicken and plastics you may come up with the new idea of a plastic chicken drinker (a device for automatically dispensing drinking water to chickens which made inventor John Leeming a millionaire in the 1960s). Or you might cross boarding-school fiction with the idea of magic and come up with Harry Potter. Or take a skateboard, remove the wheels, and use it on snow. Or if you have really diverse knowledge you might end up using spiderwebs to make a new material stronger than Kevlar (the link here was that spider webs were also used as the crosshairs in telescopic sights, and Kevlar is used for bulletproof jackets).

And it's not just inventors and writers who need innovation— we all do. Every job benefits from an innovative approach, and the bigger the pool of potential ideas you have, the better.

Permission to be creative

Lorenzo Dominguez is an intriguing man. A corporate drone, working in marketing in Manhattan, he found his life falling apart, with his marriage failing and the long commute in from New Jersey deadening. His wife had banished him to living in the basement under their suburban house and Dominguez was at the end of his tether, though anxious to keep his marriage together for the sake of his two children. His wife suggested a trial separation but living in a separate apartment was beyond his means. However, while sitting in a church in central Manhattan, he got talking to the priest, who was touched by his plight. He was given, rent-free, a small apartment right in the center of the city for three months before the property was redeveloped.

Suddenly, with time on his hands (his commute was now a matter of minutes), he was able to rekindle his old interest in photography. Every night, armed with a fairly low-end digital camera, Dominguez took to the streets of New York to take street photos. Hundreds and hundreds of photos. Pretty soon his Flickr feed was being followed by thousands of people and his pictures were featured on over 200 blogs. Prestigious photo magazines wanted to use his cut-up photos and to interview him. He was a man in demand. So what was his secret?

He gave himself permission to be creative.

Street photography as a genre grew out of the photography of Henri Cartier-Bresson and various other Leica-wielding photographers in the twentieth century. The Leica—small, easy to use, fast, and discreet—was the ultimate tool for snapping candid shots in the street, until the emergence of the high-end autofocus autoexposure camera in the late 1980s and '90s. With motor-wind automatic, even more candid shots could be taken "from the hip."

The first digital cameras were clunky beasts—and remain so if you are talking about the top-end SLRs—but in 2005 the smaller compact digital cameras started to be good enough to take creditable street photographs. Another leap in technique was now possible—except few took it, since most were stuck on their SLRs and still thinking largely in film terms. As street photography grew as a respected artistic subgenre of photography it became encrusted with "rules" that were largely derived from film days but which had become redundant with the rise of the digital compact.

Dominguez just ignored all this. He saw his camera as a tool for creativity in the crazy dream world of New York City. He realized you could push a digital camera much further than film. For one thing digital photography opened up greater possibilities of shooting at night (this was often a bit of a problem with film, as it required special developing techniques, but with digital it's easy). Instead of doing what most street photographers do—trying to make pictures look like those of the masters of yesteryear—Dominguez went out looking for beautiful pictures anywhere he could find them by twisting and tweaking his camera and developing software to the limit.

Because you can take 600 pictures in an evening with a digital camera without breaking much of a sweat, you're in a different place from film, where you might manage 200. Garry Winogrand, one of the grandmasters of street photography, used to shoot about a hundred pictures a day every day—but he left behind thousands of undeveloped cassettes. The sheer processing time for developing and printing film means the photographer eventually holds back a little. And this was one of the gaps Dominguez exploited. He photographed sequences in the street rather than single shots, and his interest in the beautiful got him out of the usual dull clichés of street photography—the gritty or ironic shots in front of billboards.

Dominguez micromastered photography almost by accident. Because he worked by day he was limited to taking photographs at night. He had no money so he used a cheap compact camera that no professional would use. He was limited to his New York neighborhood, again because of cost reasons. By narrowing it down to nighttime shots of New York taken with a cheap camera he evolved his own unique aesthetic. With these limitations he blew away many of the so-called professionals in the field (in reality, most street photographers make their living either teaching or taking more staid commercial photographs). He felt he had nothing to lose, and taking photographs was a form of therapy for him, calming his ruffled soul. We've seen before the link between play and micromastery. Because he wasn't a "pro" he was able to play with the medium. He granted himself permission to play because it simply made him feel better. And it's a short step from having permission to play to giving oneself license to create—or even a mission to create.

Lateral thinking, reverse thinking, brainstorming, and random linking

These are all the tried and tested ways to increase creativity. Lateral thinking is all about digging new holes rather than a deeper version of the hole you are already in. By thinking wide rather than deep you make new connections—the heart of any increase in creativity. Random linking is similar: just try to connect your current problem with something totally random (getting to the moon, or bananas). Simply by forcing your thoughts in this contrived way, new insights tend to emerge. Reverse thinking is another way to generate new material by simply reversing any proposition or idea that seems staid or conventional or obvious. Brainstorming involves a group effort where the emphasis is on reducing naysaying and criticism until the session has ended. The process respects the fact that creativity is usually fatally damaged by criticism and self-censoring—based on our worries about what others think—far too soon.

These techniques all evolved, it is reasonable to assert, as a response to the lack of natural material available to us, but readily available to our more polymathic forebears. Micromastery is like juicing; it simply supplies more concentrated raw materials than can be used in any of the above processes. But far more importantly it gives you the confidence to switch perspectives.

If you are a modern specialist you are deeply scared of going outside your field—and you'll fight to the death, almost, anyone trying to trespass. This develops into a rigid mind-set—you're in fight-or-flight mode—rather than open and sharing, which is how you have to be in order to be truly creative. So even if you pay lip service to the concepts of brainstorming or lateral thinking, they won't really work because you'll be too darn scared to use them. But with a few micromasteries under your belt, enabling you to flip between widely different knowledge areas, facts can start to look different and perspectives change, giving you the all-important confidence to be more creative.

Switch to "open"

Once you get used to micromastery you'll find that you are no longer seeing the world through half-shut eyes. You are slowly giving yourself permission to be interested in everything. You don't have to self-limit. And your interest won't be superficial.

Michael Merzenich, already referred to several times throughout this book, is one of the world's leading experts in stroke recovery and learning. In his research into enhanced learning for stroke victims he discovered that we have a kind of neurological switch, which is either open to learning or not. Not surprisingly, dull and unengaging things leave us closed, but being closed can become a habit. In order to be open we need to be familiar with the habit of focusing deeply and intently.

Micromastery offers us this, giving us permission to be interested in anything we choose. But why wait? Let's look at some now.

Micromastery
Central

In this section we detail thirty-nine different micromasteries. Each has four to six instructional steps. Many are illustrated to make learning even more transparent. But remember, these guides are just the start—use the video resources of the internet for anything you want to focus on more deeply. I've chosen a pretty eclectic set—and these really are just the tip of the iceberg—but for this first excursion I've focused on making and doing the things that seem to have caught my attention and held it longest. These are often traditional skills, albeit sometimes dressed up in a modern context.

In some of the micromasteries I've combined each instructional step with one of the six elements of a micromastery—the entry trick, the rub-pat barrier, background support, etc. In others, often those with fewer instructional steps, I have simply identified the various elements within the text. Either way, you have no more excuses . . .

1

Do a Line Sketch That Looks Creditable

Everyone can draw. No matter how terrible the humiliations at school I guarantee you can draw. You may have heard it said that drawing isn't about drawing, it's about looking. This will become increasingly obvious. Usually when people say they can't draw they mean they can't reach into their imaginations and draw something realistic. But this is only one aspect of drawing—one you need never approach.

1. **The way in is to copy another drawing, a line drawing you like. I found the sketches in Dan Price's offbeat books *Radical Simplicity* and *The Moonlight Chronicles* perfect for this. I also found copying sketches by the artist Egon Schiele easy and useful. But cast around until you find some line drawing you like. I say line drawing because lines come first, even if art teachers are always trying to get you using crayons and charcoal. These just produce mess and what every would-be artist wants is something that looks like art and not mess. Experienced artists manage not to make messes even with charcoal but we are not on that level yet. So get a nice technical pen—one that is smooth and black and is appealing to hold—and get copying.**

2. **The rub-pat barrier for drawing is making something look both good and recognizable. The solution is to always err on**

the side of looking good. Doesn't matter if your drawing of a excavator has wobbly lines as long as it looks kind of cool. All that messy scratching to try and get the right line is something you should try later. For now use other people's drawings, photos, and simple objects as an inspiration rather than a model. Decorate with doodly bits if it looks better. Exaggerate the good bits, leave out the stuff that looks boring. It's more enjoyable and it looks . . . better.

3. For drawing you need a sketchbook that inspires—the more expensive the better, I find. A5 is a good size for when you are out and about but maybe an A3 for when you are at home—whatever makes you want to draw. Pens follow this rule too. I find pencils boring and messy but I use them for roughing out shapes. I prefer pens with very fine tips—0.05 is a good size for me. I like Derwent pens and Berol pens. People will criticize you for using technical drawing equipment but that's nonsense—whatever makes you want to draw is good.

4. Tell yourself that you'll be happier when you have done a drawing—however basic. Artist and writer Shoo Rayner showed me how he teaches the basics of drawing: draw circles, squares, and cubes and tubes and look for these in real life—see, you can already draw them. Drawing a nice picture of a sort of cube—maybe a table or a book— is very satisfying and easy. Sign and date it for extra motivation.

5. Drawing the same thing several times isn't that boring. I do cups and glasses all the time. After a while I started to look more closely and even started the dreaded shading. It really worked. Then I looked at how the comic artist Joe Sacco shaded and I tried to copy him—another step forward. Unlike, say, photography, drawing allows an infinite number of variations in drawing the same object.

6. Experiment! The sky is the limit. Try that charcoal after all. Get messy. Branch out into watercolor—which you can ink over to get a nice effect. Copy pictures and drawings you like. I was told at school that copying was unoriginal—what nonsense. Copying is how you get started, get confident, and get going. After a while you find your own preferred style.

2

Do an Eskimo Roll

The one technique that signifies complete comfort in the water while kayaking is being competent at rolling when your boat capsizes. You're paddling along, sitting in the cockpit of your kayak, a spraydeck around your waist to stop water entering the boat. Suddenly a rogue wave tips you over. Now you are inverted, head under water, paddle in hand. If you manage to get enough traction with the paddle against the water you can roll back up and revert to being on top of, rather than under, the surface.

Many people learn how to roll only after they have done a great deal of paddling—but actually, as a classic micromastery, you can learn it even before you start using a kayak in earnest. The Eskimo roll was believed to be impossible for Europeans to master—an interesting inversion of the usual nonsense about racial inferiority—so it wasn't until the Arctic expeditions of Gino Watkins in the 1930s that learning how to roll a kayak was seen as a standard skill to acquire. It pays dividends to bear in mind the way Arctic dwellers originally rolled—they had a smallish paddle, they wore an anorak that didn't let water in anywhere—not even into their ears—and they never paddled alone, because you never know what might happen. Gino Watkins sadly ignored this last precaution and lost his life when he became too tired and cold to roll to safety. So, on that cautionary note, let's begin.

1. First off, a capsize is when your kayak inverts and, as we have mentioned, you find yourself upright underneath it with water kept out of the boat by a spraydeck around your waist. You allow your paddle to float alongside the kayak and using it as a lever pull on it to flip the boat over. By leaning forward along the front deck you create less resistance to rolling up. Experienced rollers can roll using a lifejacket or even by slapping the water with their hands. But for now, we'll use a paddle.

   The trick is in the hips. At first you'll think it is all about the paddle—but, as just stated, people roll using their hands, so the power must come from elsewhere. It does. You're upside down and your hips and backside—which are your body's center of gravity—are high up, almost above the waterline. Your thighs, feet, and knees are braced against the canoe either directly or through straps—which allows direct transmission of a hip flick into the shell of the boat. Think of swinging a hula hoop around your hips. Now imagine flipping that hoop up in the air with one hip. With that image in mind get to a dock or jetty or pool that has an edge you can grab hold of, and capsize the body of the boat while you remain above water hanging on to the edge. You are now in a position to use your hips to flip the boat upright. You will learn to feel the full connection from hip movement to boat. At first you'll be heaving on the dock edge but after a while only the lightest of touches will be needed. You are now ready to try with a lifejacket or swimming float instead of the dock. It's floating, so it's a little different, but the essence is the same. After the lifejacket move on to the paddle—you let it lie alongside the boat on the surface and pull hard down on it, initiating a stroke downward. You're

pulling on the paddle so it won't move that far through the water—remember you are using it like a bar to help right the boat. The harder and faster you slap the water with it, the more it will act as if it is hitting

something solid rather than liquid. At the EXACT SAME TIME use a sudden hip movement to rock the boat the same way as the paddle pull-down suggests. You'll surge to the surface.

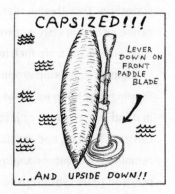

2. The rub-pat barrier is matching the hip swing with the paddle pull/slap. The smarter the coordination of the two, the less force you need in either. You need to work on the dockside to feel the real connection between the hips, the boat, and the pulled-on object—be it hands, lifejacket, dock, or paddle.

If you neglect this and simply roll again and again you can spend weeks with only limited success—whereas starting the way I've suggested can have you rolling in half an hour.

3. Get the gear that suits you—makes you feel like doing rolls. A small kayak is less important than one you fit well, with no slack between flexing your body and moving the boat. Wear earplugs—constantly going under will ram water into your ears in a most unpleasant way. The original rollers wore an anorak over their heads—which you can replicate with a wet-suit helmet. Wear a wet suit or dry suit or do it on a very warm day—getting cold will really damage your learning curve. Plenty of time to roll in icy water when you have mastered the technique. Wear a helmet in case of underwater obstructions. The paddle I favor is unfeathered and quite small. This means both blades are in the same plane while on the water's surface, providing a little more to pull off. But you may find feathered blades are better.

4. Fear of going over and staying under is the biggest worry facing a kayaker—whether on a rapid flowing river or in the sea or crossing a big windy lake. If you can't roll you'll always be a little nervous. And if you are attempting very turbulent water just knowing how to roll will improve your paddling skills no end.

5. To gamify learning to roll you can make it a party piece whenever you go out kayaking. As long as you have

your earplugs in—another "plug" for Doc's Proplugs—
you'll be fine.

6. After micromastering a roll with a conventional double
    paddle, try with a single paddle. Then try with your hands.
    Try with a fully laden kayak. Try with a two-person
    kayak. The next step is to try to roll an open canoe with
    buoyancy in it.

3

Find the Depth of a Well or a Deep Hole

Everyone likes a good deep mysterious hole in the ground. It could be an old mineshaft, a cave, a well, or even a lift shaft (though you have to be careful dropping stones down lift shafts). Yes, stones—that is the secret of finding just how deep that hole is.

1. The trick is knowing the formula—a very simple one that dates back to Galileo. It relies on the fact that all objects, whatever their size, accelerate toward the earth at the same rate—9.8 meters per second per second. (Speed is measured in meters per second, acceleration in the increase in speed—hence meters per second per second.) Gravity is the cause of the acceleration, and as long as you don't choose a feather or a very light stone you'll get a good result. (A feather does drop at the same rate as a stone if there is no air—but air resistance is minimal on a small heavy stone.) Now 9.8 is a bit clumsy so let's round it up to 10. Next you'll need a watch or a way of counting off seconds. I say "one barra barra, two barra barra, three barra barra" and it's pretty accurate—accurate enough to get a well's depth to the nearest few meters. So you release the stone and start counting and only stop when you hear the plop. The depth is half of the acceleration (which is half of 10, which is 5) multiplied by the time squared. So if you time a three-second drop it's 5×3×3=45 meters deep.

2. Is there a barrier to doing this? Not really. Getting the timing accurate is the main thing. You can use a stopwatch if you like.

3. A good stone is hard to find. Well, maybe not that hard, but it's worth getting one. Sometimes holes and caves have updrafts and a tiny stone will catch in the wind. A massive great boulder is a tad over the top and might hit the walls of the well, which would mess with the time. A stone a little bit smaller than a golf ball will work fine.

4. The payoff for stone dropping is the intense satisfaction gained from knowing the exact depth of a deep crevice, hole, or puncture in the earth's surface. It is in our nature to want to explore and know things we perhaps should not, and there is something a little miraculous in the idle and even careless gesture of dropping a stone down a well resulting in a precise measure of its depth. Something only otherwise to be discovered by the painstaking and tedious process of lowering a weight on a measuring line.

5. To gamify stone dropping make it competitive. You'll need a length of string that you premeasure and lower with a weight attached into the well or hole. In other cases you may find that the depth of the well is already known—the person who gets the closest to the official figure is the winner. Obviously you have to exercise a bit of caution and common sense. A stone dropped on the head of a caver or someone

down a hole can kill or maim, so make sure the hole is clear before you do it.

6. This is one of the most basic experiments in physics but it leads into the whole realm of measuring things that perplex us on country walks and other excursions, when someone might ask "How wide is that river?" or "How high is that tree?" followed sometimes by the offer of a wager. Well, heights and widths are just as easy to compute from rudimentary tools and simple geometry, something that the practical amateur physicist might like to pursue, having tasted success in well-depth measuring.

4

Chop Through a Log (or Even a Tree)

We live in ecologically minded times—thank goodness—but, even so, there comes a time when some trees need to be felled either because of old age or disease or simply because there are too many of them. You could use a chainsaw (boo!), which is a bit boring and ordinary, or you could use a felling ax—which isn't as straightforward as it looks.

1. Let's start with the log, lying on the ground, probably too heavy to move—now, how do you cut through it? What usually happens is that the novice lumberjack hacks into it with carefree and ebullient abandon, only to discover that once he has cut a small V he has to spend much of his energy widening the gap so that he can go deeper. This is time-consuming and makes it almost impossible to cut through a log much wider than a foot. However, the trick is to mark out a section as wide as the log is deep. You make a chop on the right and then one on the left, and then pry out the chip of wood in between. If it's a two-foot-wide tree, then the chip will be two feet long. You then repeat this, making cuts to the right and left that are a little closer—again the chip comes flying out. It's very satisfying to see so much wood going with so little work, and it explains how the lumberjacks of yore used to deforest the planet so easily . . .

2. The rub-pat barrier is not that high, once you have a good ax and provided the wood isn't too hard. The main balance is between force on the ax and letting the weight of the ax do the work. If you whale on the ax you'll tire very quickly. Anyone watching wood chopping done by traditional tribeswomen in the Himalayas will see the almost boneless way they chop—using their strength to raise the machete or ax and letting it cut using just its own weight plus a bit of accelerating whip. Getting a "feel" for an ax is about letting the 2+ lb of weight in the head do the cutting, not your straining arms. Always look where you want the ax to land. Simply focusing hard on a specific spot on the log will be enough for you to hit the right spot.

3. The ax you need is for cutting and not splitting. As most people only use an ax for splitting, the wide wedge-shaped-head axes are very common—but aren't much use for cutting into a log or tree. To cut deeply into the wood you need a narrow head, just as a fileting knife is narrow. How big an ax

depends on what size logs you want to cut through. If you are going for felling trees more than a foot across you'll need a full-size ax like the Gränsfors American felling ax, which weighs in at nearly 5 lb—more than enough to chop through any log you want.

4. Chopping through a log is very satisfying—and, when done correctly, the chips you pry out can be used as kindling—so nothing is wasted. You can then split the log using a wedge or a splitting ax—thus having a whole firewood-generating operation without recourse to the dreaded chainsaw. You'll also get a terrific workout, which develops strength and coordination.

5. If you have a wood-burning stove or a fireplace it's very easy to use an ax instead of a saw. The ritual of sharpening and caring for the ax—which is much easier than it is with a saw—makes a further enticement for continuing to practice and improve.

6. Experimenting with an ax sounds a bit dangerous, but the ax is the preferred tool of many outdoorsmen like Ray Mears and Mors Kochanski. A smaller ax can be used for carving and even whittling, while a larger ax can be used to fell enough logs to make a shelter or even a cabin. The traditional pointed ends of a cabin's logs mimic those chopped by an ax rather than sawn through.

5

Learn How to Climb a Rope

Rope climbing is not often called upon except in the obscure world of the tree climber and tree surgeon. Mountaineers mostly don't know how to climb ropes; they use special ascending devices instead. In the gym there is sometimes a thick, rough rope to climb, and some might manage it. For others even this relatively simple ascent is as mysterious and difficult as the Indian rope trick. And yet rope climbing is a useful combination of coordination and strength; it may even save your life if you find yourself trapped in some dark recess where only a rope's length can save you. And there is never enough time to knot the rope like in a children's adventure novel. It might be a case of climb or die . . .

1. **Thick ropes are easier to climb as the friction between rope and feet—the key trick—is greater. A thin rope typically found in tree-surgery-type climbing is around 13 mm—half an inch—and not great for hanging from. A gripper knot or ascender device can be slid up the rope and hung off as you move your feet up. Either way the key is in the feet, not the hands. As mentioned in "Dynamic Learning," you have to wrap the rope around both feet in an "S" shape, the top foot in the top part of the "S" pressing down hard on the other foot in the lower part of the "S." Boots or sturdy trainers work better than bare feet with thin ropes; thicker ropes allow thinner footwear and need less wraparound. The idea**

of looping the rope around the foot is to create a very powerful brake, which moves up the rope when the braking top foot is off, but remains locked on the rope when the braking foot is on. You hang by your hands for the brief moment that you slide your feet up the rope. Knees now bent, you apply the "brake" and stand up, straightening your knees and gaining height. The hands and arms are for hanging off only, not for gaining height—that is done by the knees straightening.

2. The rub-pat barrier is one of coordination. You have to hang for a second or two from your hands while your feet entwine the rope and slide upward. You then tighten the coil of rope between your feet to lock yourself in position. This allows you to slide your

WITH A THICK ROPE

Making the 'S'

WITH A THINNER ROPE

Move foot across as a brake

A FASTER WAY TO CLIMB A THINNER ROPE

Use this foot to stamp on rope on top of other foot

hands up the rope to repeat the process. Sliding up and locking out efficiently greatly reduces the strain on the hands—really tree climbing is about coordination and skill rather than brute strength. Allowing the rope to travel around your feet without it coming off is part of the skill.

3. Start with a thick rope and progress to thinner ropes. If you aim to use the ½-inch tree-climbing rope, practice by hanging from an ascender and using your feet to slide up and down so that you get the hang of it.

4. Rope climbing is a great all-body workout. Though modern gyms may lack the old ropes dangling from the ceiling, there has been something of a revival of rope climbing as it is a favorite of military training. Because it builds upper body strength as well as calf- and foot-muscle strength and coordination, it's a unique exercise.

5. You can time yourself going up the rope. Indeed, if you get good, there are rope-climbing contests you can enter. At first you might fear that you'll run out of strength, but after some practice this idea seems absurd. With the right technique rope climbing requires much less energy than it seems to. At that point you can start loading yourself with weights or tree-climbing gear to make it harder.

6. Tree climbing has its dangers—I fell out of a tree once and broke my arm—but pursued carefully and with the right gear and climbing partners you should be able to find a safety

margin that works for you. Rope climbing might lead
you into the heady world of climbing giant trees—over
three hundred feet (a hundred meters) tall in the U.S.
and Australia. This opens up a whole new world seen
from on high.

6

Surf Standing Up

Surfing is the activity that signifies existential freedom more than any other. You're out there, in the moment, riding the wave and living the life. Never mind that in a few moments your nose will be dragging along the sea bed as the board gets tossed by a giant breaker—for a few brief moments you were up there with the gods. If you think you're too old to take it up, check out the book *Surf Mama* by Wilma Johnson (Beautiful Books, 2011) or Google "pensioner surfers" . . .

1. **The entry trick—before you get out into the water—is to practice popping up onto your feet and not your knees. Using knees develops into a bad habit that is hard to break—and it isn't any easier to get up either. Start by lying face-down on the ground, without a board. Think of yourself as in press-up position (but it helps to have your feet flat out at the back as if flippering—not with toes curled under and gripping the**

floor). Do a rubbish press-up with your tummy still on the ground and keep looking ahead. Really arch your back before popping up and standing with your front foot under your shoulder. Don't worry about your flippered out toes—they will obey the will to stand! Angle your body to face either right or left, but keep your head facing forward. The feet should be at around forty-five degrees or so on the board— the main thing is to be in a balanced pose. When popping up, keep looking forward and not down as head movement will upset your balance. Once you've begun to teach your body the move, transfer to a bouncy bed. Lay a surfboard on top, dangle your toes off the end, place your hands flat, arch up, and pop into position. The bed will wobble and simulate the water better than doing it on hard ground. When popping up feels natural(ish), get out into the waves.

2. The rub-pat barrier is synchronizing the upward push with the movement of the board on the wave. Too soon and you'll have no stability; too late and you'll have lost control of the

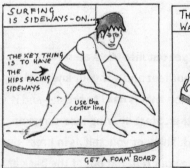

SURFING IS SIDEWAYS-ON...

THE KEY THING IS TO HAVE THE HIPS FACING SIDEWAYS

Use the center line

GET A FOAM BOARD

THE 'CHICKEN WING' - ANOTHER WAY TO POP

This swoops under to become the front foot

eyes forward

This remains in position as the BACK foot.

board. The moment when the board begins to slip away and you feel the force of the wave surge you forward is a forgiving moment. You can push into the board and this causes further sliding down the wave rather than a wobble. Using this moment of stability makes it easier to get to your feet on the board.

3. Get earplugs—Doc's Proplugs, of course—wear a wetsuit—a full-length one, if you have the slightest problem with cold water. The whole point is to enjoy being out there and not be shivering and desperate. If you are happy in the water you'll find you spend less time in it. Get a board that is fairly long. Cool boards are really short but the longer boards are more stable and easier to stand up on. Foam boards, also looked down on, are actually brilliant for starting on. Lastly—go where there are good waves breaking some way offshore. Learning in tricky waves makes it just that much more difficult. Taking a course after you have practiced popping up will give you great confidence as the instructors will know the good spots for beginners to surf.

4. Surfing is a great way to visit some of the more remote spots in the world. From Norway to Angola there are people searching out wilderness beaches to surf and enjoy. Surfing puts you right in the moment—it's a great antidote to routine and dull office life. Even if you're only in the water for a few minutes, it seems a much longer time. And then if you are in for hours, the time can just fly by.

5. Surfing is addictive. Feed the addiction by finding some surfing pals. Be happy going in for a short time, coming out for a coffee from a flask, and going back in again. No need to be macho and keep going when it isn't fun any more. Go for longer and longer bursts.

6. Surfing developed in Hawaii with two versions—stand-up paddle boarding and full-body surfing. Stand-up paddle boarding is one way to get into surfing without knowing how to pop up. On a paddle board you can surf even tiny waves and get used to standing on a board in water. You can also practice popping up on a paddle board in still water—better than practicing on land as it is more realistic.

7

Talk for Fifteen Minutes about Any Subject

Public speaking—famously more feared than death itself—is without doubt a key skill in most jobs. To be able to speak on any subject without preparation seems impossible to the uninitiated, and yet as soon as you have read the following instructions you too will be able to manage it. As micromasteries go this is one of my favorites, and we have the inventor of most modern improvisation games, Keith Johnstone,* to thank for it.

1. **The main trick is to describe what you are doing, what you are feeling, what you are thinking—RIGHT NOW. So if you are standing there feeling nervous and unprepared tell the audience you are nervous and unprepared. If you have been given the subject of Chinese vases of the Later Han dynasty, tell them the precise limits of your knowledge. How little or how much you know. What the subject brings to mind or makes you feel. This is not simply waffling, it is the precise relating of your state of mind and as such is perfectly germane to the subject. If people start shuffling their feet and leaving, tell the audience that too—always good for a few laughs.**

* Keith Johnstone, *Impro: Improvisation and the Theatre* (Methuen Drama, 2007).

2. When you feel stuck for words, ask the audience. There is almost certainly someone or even several people who know more than you do about this difficult subject you have been tasked with talking about. Ask with enthusiasm and treat the volunteers with great respect and courtesy. Ask their names and occupations and where they live—we all love a bit of biography. Get them to come down to the front and reassure them. Then question them carefully to elicit what they know. After they are done, instigate a heartfelt round of applause. Avoid like the plague the easy and sarcastic comment—these folks just saved your bacon!

3. You are now into the final straight and the third lifesaving trick is to REVERSE the emotion. Rumble up to the revelation that Chinese vases actually make you sick, that they are pointless and useless, symbols of degenerate and antidemocratic practices . . . and so on. Reversing the emotion can bring out a whole lot of new and unsuspected material.

4. Being fearless at public speaking is a wonderful thing. Think of all those parties, dinners, weddings, business presentations, sales meetings, illustrated talks, and Oscar acceptance speeches that will no longer FILL YOU WITH FEAR. You'll find that people will actually laugh at even half-amusing things you say—simply by being relaxed and using the audience, rather than feverishly trying to remember stuff, you will seem funny to them.

5. Practice whenever you can. You can do it at the bar or at a party. People might find it a bit odd but this is the way to build even more confidence and humor—which is often a key part of a successful speech.

6. Public speaking might lead you into the incredible world of improv. This is far more than the type of thing you see on *Whose Line Is It Anyway?* Improv is about making your fellow improvisers look good rather than showing off yourself. When everyone is making everyone look good, all sorts of magic can happen.

8

Lay a Brick Wall

One thing that sets the dabblers apart from the more dedicated home-improver is the ability to lay bricks. I mean, how hard can it be? Well, many try and fail—but there really is no reason. The idea that you have to be apprenticed at fifteen to learn the dark art of bricklaying is nonsense. The celebrated polymath Winston Churchill was inordinately proud of the still-standing wall he built at his country retreat, Chartwell—so take inspiration from his example and get to laying! Like all micromasteries, this could lead on to far bigger and grander projects—but everything starts with the simple laying of one brick on top of another to make, at its most basic, a wall half a brick wide (i.e. bricks laid lengthways, one brick in thickness). This is the best thing to start with (rather than the usual test piece, a barbecue stand) as the work is not complicated by adding slabs and grills.

1. **The entry trick, the thing that will get you up and running, is the cement you use. Notice I said cement and not mortar. Lime mortar is a wonderful bonding agent that allows the building to breathe and even move a little, but it dries more slowly (while appearing to dry out faster) and is trickier to use. It's the next level up—perfectly attainable once you have mastered using cement, sand, and the all-important plasticizer. To be really certain start with plasticizer— bought from a DIY store. (Though dishwashing liquid is**

often used instead, proper plasticizer is much better and more durable.) Mix up the sand—must be bricklayer's soft sand as it has some clay in it—in four parts to one part cement. Then add the plasticizer following the instructions. Do this in a bucket—easier at first than on a traditional board. Then add water bit by bit, stirring with your trowel. You want to really break a sweat to get a soft ice-cream or smooth peanut-butter texture.

2. Work up to this slowly—the mix is the key. This is the rub-pat barrier—too sloppy and the bricks will sink and misalign under the weight of the bricks above. But too stiff and the bricks won't adhere and everything will be dry and crumbly, and it's much harder work to get them level in stiff cement. When using the bucket and adding water, don't make too much—it's better to get the consistency right. Cement in a bucket won't dry out as fast as cement on a board, but you can always spray water on the top to keep it moist. And on a hot day you can wet the bricks before laying them. All this keeps the mix in the right state. Now slop some cement out onto the concrete base—always have a flat concrete surface to build on—and notch a running "V" down the center of the splodge of cement. How big a splodge? A good trowelful—the aim is to get the brick sitting on about a half-inch (1 cm) of level cement. Which means the initial lump of mix with its "V" should be about double that in thickness. You can angle the sides in a bit too so that it doesn't splurge out too much. With the brick on it should not sink until pushed and tapped down with the trowel. Use a spirit level

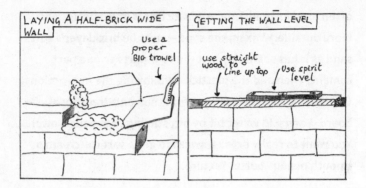

to make sure it is perfectly square and use a notched measuring stick to make sure it is the right height.

3. Tools and materials are crucial to making it all work. Plasticizer and brick sand will really help with the mix. Get a proper bricklayer's trowel, not one of those little DIY tile trowels. Use a string line running the whole length of the wall to get a constant idea of the height the course of brickwork should be. For a first attempt it is somewhat easier to build between two existing dead-straight supports or walls— filling the gap means you only have to worry about the lean of the wall and whether it is level.

4. Winston Churchill was so proud of his wall he'd show it off to all visitors who came to Chartwell. People are impressed by anyone who can build a wall, even a low one, and this favorable attention should spur you on. But, more than this, there is the almost primitive sense of achievement in "raising walls." You are engaged in building the basics of a

shelter, one of humankind's most fundamental needs. Perhaps some of that ancestral imprinting makes wall making so addictive.

5. Just making one wall allows for great repetition of the basic act of laying a brick. You can focus on making each laid brick a perfect one. If it isn't, no matter, in a few seconds you'll have yet another chance to improve your skills.

6. There is no end to the experimental possibilities. From the classic simple "stretcher bond" of bricks laid on top of each other in a single thickness, each one overlapping by half a brick, you can progress to all manner of fancy decorative styles of bricklaying. There are all manner of different, even colored, mortars. You could even build a house . . .

9

Write Dialogue

Everyone is a writer these days. The mass use of computers and the internet in almost every home makes us all potential authors. Whether we're any good or not is almost irrelevant. The fact is— if you want to write and publish a novel or script, you can. And some novels by outsider authors—like *Fifty Shades of Grey* by E. L. James—can become huge successes. Every novel and screenplay needs dialogue—and this is where people demonstrate their skill in naked glory or ignominy. Even some rather well-regarded writers think dialogue is about conflict or Pinter-style parallel monologues. But there is much more to it than that.

1. **The incredible entry trick of writing dialogue is status. Dialogue that is *dramatically* interesting reveals status differences. Perhaps we are attuned to this for evolutionary reasons. This doesn't mean higher status is good, it just means an attunement to status better enables one to survive. So, to write great dialogue, first assign status levels to both the interlocutors. This is not social status but rather human-interactive status—for example Hugh Grant may talk like an upper-class Englishman but he acts low status, hence the way he has problems with anyone more assertive than he is. A motor mechanic who is physically imposing and unwilling to play second fiddle to anyone will have higher status in a conversation than an aristocrat dropping off his**

Audi for a once-over. So before you start writing any dialogue, ask who is the higher-status individual in this time and place. You might think they are equal status—in that case do status switching. One acts high status for a while and then is toppled—maybe by a joke—and then the other gets the high-status position. Friends signify their intimacy by treating status as a joke, or by switching status for comic effect. One sign of high-status play is the absence of a sense of humor during a status challenge. A high-status player will fight rather than relinquish his or her status. Which is where the drama comes in.

2. It's important to remember this: high-status people can be happy and positive or mean and negative—and likewise for mid- and low-status people. We often assume that high status means gloomy and curt—the clichéd view of the upper classes in lots of movies—but a high-spirited and happy high-status person is also possible. The rub-pat barrier is balancing realism of dialogue—which is made easier once you have status involved—with meaningful content. Sometimes you have to show people talking nonsense— that's fine—but eventually the dialogue will have to convey meaningful content. Doing this without being heavy-handed is the balancing act, again made far easier by framing it as a status interaction rather than an information download.

3. Don't think character, think relationship when you are writing dialogue. That's where preset relationships come in handy: mother–son, servant–master, teacher–pupil. A

relationship is what interests us, not a bizarre character. A psycho serial killer with all his grotesque rituals will hold our attention for about five minutes, but give him some victims who know him (but don't know he's a psycho) and a policeman on his trail, and we'll be hooked for hours.

4. Think of people you know and consider their relationship in terms of status. Who dominates and how? Who submits and how? Then imagine a dialogue between them on any subject from football to magic. See how it moves back and forth, one deferring, the other showing off knowledge. Or maybe they take turns in being dominant.

5. Take a look at Desmond Morris's *Manwatching** to get more ideas about status as it concerns the human primate. If in doubt about dialogue, ask yourself who is the bigger gorilla in any conversation and proceed from there.

6. Some people are stuck with the high-status role all the time. Others can alternate. Some only do low status in intimate surroundings or in the presence of someone famous. Aristotle Onassis—someone whose status was higher than almost anyone's—used to act as a very attentive servant to Winston Churchill when the statesman came aboard his yacht. This was because Churchill could only "do" high status. To avoid a clash Onassis switched to playing low status.

---

* Desmond Morris, *Manwatching: A Field Guide to Human Behavior* (H. N. Abrams, 1977).

10

Make a Clay Skull

Ever wanted to be a sculptor? A real sculptor, I mean, as in realistic, making figures that actually look like someone? It doesn't get more demanding than working for Madame Tussauds, where world-class sculptor Mike Wade learned his trade before becoming a freelance maker of wax lookalikes. He's made replicas of Princess Diana, George Clooney, and Nelson Mandela for leading waxwork collections around the world. What particularly intrigued me is that he did not go to art school, preferring instead to learn on the job at Madame Tussauds—the old way—watching an older expert and then trying to emulate them. Mike immediately got what micromastery was about; he suggested the best example for head sculpture was making skulls out of clay or even Plasticine.

1. The head is a complex object—there are ears, nose, and chin, all of which protrude. There are eyes that need to be depicted as either open or shut. Not to mention the shape of the head and the neck. It can get confusing. Which is where skull sculpting comes in. The skull that lurks beneath the skin is the chassis, the bedrock of our faces and all our features. But instead of a nose, eyes, and ears we have holes—leaving you to concentrate on the shape of the head and the jaw. By limiting yourself it's so much easier to get an artist's understanding of what heads are really like.

2. Making the skull lifelike is the trap many fall into—so make it skull-like! The barrier to surmount is balancing lifelike qualities with making something that works as a whole. The first step, then, is to make a skull that looks good. You can play around and make it look like a horror skull, the skull of a partly decayed monster, a shrunken-head skull. Just getting used to doing skulls will build an awareness of what is important in making them.

3. For making skulls you want to keep, use a quick-drying, non-firing clay such as Das. If you just want to play use Plasticine. Get the kind used by sculptors that is all gray or brown. You can also use ordinary modeling clay, which comes in cheap 10 lb tubs from art supply shops. You can hollow out the skull to help it dry.

4. Skulls are fun things to make into lanterns for Halloween. They amuse children—unless they are too realistic, in which case you might find you have caused a nightmare or two . . .

5. Build up a skull collection. Carry the Plasticine with you all the time so you can fashion skulls of people you are looking at. Get used to imagining what someone's skull would look like. It's a good way to get better at sculpting, which, like other forms of realistic art, is all about looking harder and more clearly at something rather than having some special artistic skills.

6. Try skulls from different animals. Get hold of some skulls to model. I tried a ram's skull that I found while walking in Scotland. After a while you'll find you inevitably graduate from the skull to what lies above it—a real human face. Since you will be so familiar with its chassis and underpinnings, its range of movement and dimensions, your heads will look good from the start.

11

Bake Excellent Artisan Bread

There are few better ways into the arcane world of baking than making bread—excellent bread up to the highest artisanal standards. The good news is that making bread has only a few variables and there are several entry tricks which will elevate your loaf, causing it literally to rise above the rest . . .

Bread is very, very simple—but easy to mess up if you are in a rush. The supermarket variety is made rapidly and needs lots of extra chemicals to make this happen. But using time and a canny knowledge of temperature you can achieve far better results with no additives. There is a lot of good bread-making advice out there, but it is apt to be confusing. This micromastery aims to remove that confusion.

1. **Time is the first entry trick—set aside an entire day for your first foray into serious bread making. This doesn't mean you can't do lots of other things—you can; most of bread making is waiting for it to rise—but you need to be around and, most importantly, not in a hurry. Have a book you want to read at the kitchen table ready to pick up when the bread starts to do its thing.**

    The second entry trick is: keep it wet. No one likes wet sticky dough getting everywhere, so the temptation is to cover the kneading board and your hands with dry flour to stop this. But over-adding flour is the single biggest cause of

heavy, undercooked bread. Instead lightly oil the kneading board (olive oil is good), the bowl, and even your hands to reduce the sticking factor. But "stick" to the correct proportions—use a scale and, even if the dough seems too wet, don't be tempted to keep adding flour.

The third great entry trick is to use super-strong Canadian organic flour. This can be used straight or mixed 50/50 with ordinary strong bread flour to produce a loaf with outstanding flavor. Right from the word go your loaves will be of a higher standard. You'll also need water and just a hint of olive oil. Purists can leave out the oil, but it helps the loaf form a nice crust. Make sure the water you add is warm. Yeast can be standard instant yeast—the dried stuff. Later you can experiment with wet yeast and sourdoughs.

While mixing the flour, water, and yeast you will need to add salt. Do so when the yeast has already been thoroughly mixed in and make sure the salt is lightly scattered as too much salt kills yeast. Then you need to knead. Pummel and stretch for at least ten minutes. After kneading for what seems like an age, break off a piece about the size of a big marble and stretch it out so that it is see-through. It should be like chewing gum at this stage—plastic enough to stretch thin.

2. The rub-pat barrier in bread making is balancing time and temperature. To some extent they are related—if the air temperature is low you can proof the loaf by leaving it much longer. But yeast imparts more flavor when the temperature is higher (confusingly, other flavors come out with longer, cooler proofing sessions—this is one area for great

experimentation). But above 104°F the yeast dies. The optimum for standard proofing/flavor is around 85°F. This is best achieved by setting the oven to 120°F and then switching it off when you put the loaf in. The loaf and its container will absorb quite a bit of heat, leaving a nice average of around 85°F to make the loaf rise. You know when the proofing is finished when you can stick two fingers into the mix and it doesn't pop back out, or pops out only very, very slowly. Give it time to proof—but remember, each time you open the oven door you are letting out the heat and the process will slow down.

Once it has risen, knead again for a further ten minutes. Then, more proofing—this time inside the baking tins and again in a warm but switched-off oven. Allow the bread to increase in size by 150–200 percent. Allow an hour, though it may be ready before then—you can check by using the finger test again. Now put it in the oven at 425°F. If you put a tray of water in the bottom of the oven the crust will be finer.

3. We have mentioned super-strong flour, but getting flour you trust and love is a key part of the process. Go online and check out the various flour mills you can buy from direct. Organic is best for ridding you of the "I'm eating chemicals" feeling that is apt to spoil even the most innocent of eating pleasures. A good big board for kneading the bread. Good, easy-to-use scales. These aid calibration—if you keep the quantities the same you will discover what variables are important.

4. The payoff from good bread is immediate and very gratifying. EVERYONE prefers it to supermarket stuff. Slice and freeze some as soon as it is cool—use this for toast every morning.

5. Get into the habit of making bread once a week to keep the house fully stocked. As mentioned, stick to the exact same proportions for ingredients but alter times and temperatures to see what effect they have.

6. Later, start to experiment by altering the quantity of super-strong flour you use, the time for proofing—some artisan bread requires twenty-four hours in the fridge. Try sourdough, different yeasts, different flours, and adding olives, raisins, and other goodies to your mix.

12

Make a Sword Hum Through the Air

A delightfully obscure skill—swinging a sword and causing it to make a thrumming noise as it descends at high speed, presumably to chop someone's arm, head, or leg off. But there are plenty of martial arts where metal and wooden swords—called *bokken*—are used for practice. And since the correct hum, signifying the correct hold, is transferable to any remotely similar object—from an ax to a golf club—the mastery overlap is considerable. It is also quite satisfying when a young relative hands you a toy sword or even a stick masquerading as a sword and you can make that telltale humming noise (of which Luke's lightsaber noise is but a pale imitation).

1. **The trick that will get you started is to hold the sword gently. Swords tend to excite people and consequently are held far too tightly. The great seventeenth-century Japanese swordsman Musashi used to approach opponents gingerly and allow his sword tip to touch theirs. If it was rigidly held he would fight, if he detected it was held in a relaxed way he would flee . . .**

The entry trick is: hold the sword gently, not tightly

make that satisfying thrumming sound . . .

Imagine holding something living and a little fragile that might escape your grip. Now drop and relax your shoulders and think of accelerating the pommel, the end of the handle (which is sometimes weighted), pulling it down and toward you, allowing the weight of the sword to start the motion so that you, utilizing this momentum and the leverage, can actually make the sword descend so fast it cuts the air and makes a hum.

2. The rub-pat barrier to sword cutting is that you need to use strength, but you also need to be relaxed. This is why sword cutting is the basis of many exercise routines in such martial arts as aikido. By endlessly cutting on thin air you build the right reflexes and muscles needed to throw people and apply sudden pressure to their bodies. The way through the barrier is to practice as tensely as you can—call that 10, then go to 9, 8, and so on. Eventually you will feel a sweet spot of relaxed shoulders but contained and ready power.

3. Get a wooden sword online or from a martial arts shop. These were actually used by poor samurai instead of real swords—and there are accounts of people with wooden swords defeating the real thing. They are good to practice with and after a little work you'll easily be able to make that blade hum.

4. Sword cutting builds your lats, but also works as a kind of meditation. Standing in the dawn light doing endless cuts down, across, and diagonally both calms and improves focus.

There is something about having a sword in your hands that really stimulates a strong state of concentration.

5. You can obviously move on to learning a sword style—there are many traditional ones in Japan. Or you can try making other things hum, maybe a baseball bat . . .

13

Make String from Nettles

You are in the wilderness, or even your own back garden, and you desperately need a piece of string. You might want to fashion an impromptu fishing line or make a guy rope. To be able to make rope and string from natural materials is one of the basic arts of primitive living. Once micromastered, it is useful and enjoyable, and provides a gentle way into more testing wilderness skills.

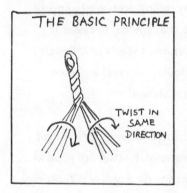

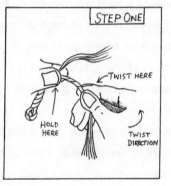

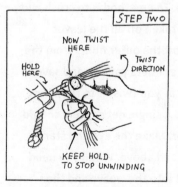

1. **The entry trick can be practiced with ordinary string. Once you know it, the transfer to natural materials is easy. The basic principle of all rope making is to twist the strands one way and use their unraveling to twist**

them both together. You can start with a piece of string doubled. Hold the "eye" (the bend with the two ends coming out) tightly and simply rub the two loose ends in parallel between your fingers. Try to increase the tightness of their weave. Then, without letting go of the eye, let the ends unravel and twist together—it's like magic—the very tension you put into tightening strand now unleashes itself in winding the two strands together.

2. The rub-pat barrier is holding the strands in one hand and rotating them in your fingers (or on your thigh) like someone rolling a cigar. You need a steady rolling pressure to ensure that you impart enough twist so that when it unravels it re-forms as rope. One way to surmount this is to roll each strand in turn, pinching it so it doesn't unravel and then manually twisting it over the next strand.

3. Now is the time to start using the nettles or inner fibers of bark or even grass as a strand material. Nettles are good as they are plentiful and provide strong cordage—easily stringy enough to make into fishing line. The method is to crush and flatten the nettle stalks (having taken off all the leaves wearing gloves). You then strip off the outer fibers from the woody inner pith. It is these outer fibers you dry and save to make cordage. Wet your fingers as you twist it to rehydrate the fibers enough to grip better. A single nettle stem should provide about four strips of fiber. Make the eye and start twisting them as we have described above. When you need to add a new fiber just overlap it into the weave and then

start twisting it with the other strand. You don't want the strand lengths to be even as two overlaps next to each other weaken the cord.

4. Like the hand drill, making cord is a major survival skill and as such is both useful and capable of eliciting interest from all ages. I've found it a good thing to teach children as they often try to make rope from grass and stalks—with this they can produce something that actually works.

5. Ray Mears challenges people to make a thirty-foot (ten-meter) length of nettle cord when they go on his courses. It's long enough to be a real challenge and also to produce a useful length of string or cord. Making thirty-feet's worth you are bound to learn the best way to keep it even in diameter and ensure a tightness of weave.

6. Almost anything can be made into cord. I was in Indonesia and saw an elderly man pull strands of grass out from the thatched roof and start to roll them on his thigh to make rope. In a few minutes he had a beautifully even and sturdy piece of cord. You can experiment with grass, the inner bark of pine and willow, and also threads and strings you want to weave into thicker rope.

14

Sing Solo, Even If You Are Tone Deaf

Along with public speaking, singing solo for the nongifted is pretty high up in the terror stakes. Often you have to be a bit drunk to manage it—and that only messes with your ability to hit the notes. I am a truly untalented singer so I took a course called "Singing for the Tone Deaf." The teacher not only got us all singing on a nationwide TV show eventually—he had us singing solo by the end of the first lesson.

1. **Our teacher's success was based on getting everyone to first make animal noises. You could make any kind of noise, of course, but animal noises offer lots of variety—try chimp, cow, sheep, whale. Once you get pretty used to being some kind of animal, turn up the energy. This is the key entry trick. When bad singers go out of tune, what do they do? They give it less oomph and less energy and consequently go even more out of tune. You have to learn to do the reverse. When you sense you are losing the note—pump out more power from your stomach. It is the center from which committed singing comes. Bad singers are used to warbling from their chests and throats, and though the talented can shift their voice into different locations, when you start you must rely on your stomach as the organ of power and source of all energy in singing. By compressing and tightening your stomach muscles you'll have a much bigger and stronger**

supply of air. Try making a cow noise from just the head and then add the stomach power—see the huge difference. Now add that power when you sing.

2. The barriers to singing better are mainly psychological. No one wants to look a fool so we stop singing in public. With less practice you get less confident and use less power. And go more out of tune. Very few people are truly tone deaf (a severe condition usually noticeable because the speaking voice of the sufferer is affected), so becoming a better singer is really about practice and knowing that the more energy you use, the easier it is. You can even sing quietly—but throttle back the power by using your stomach muscles.

3. Karaoke is good for practice—as long as there is some backing music. Don't attempt "Bridge over Troubled Water," as I did on a first visit to a karaoke box in Tokyo—there's no music to hide behind! Pick some old classics you actually like and sing them a lot. Show tunes and musicals are always good.

4. Never again will you be embarrassed at a birthday party or carol service.

5. You might consider joining other incompetent singers in a "tone deaf" choir. Or maybe learn folk singing. The quavering timbre used by old folk singers is a good way of hitting the right note at some point or another. Tell yourself repeatedly that Bob Dylan can't sing and that has never

stopped him. Go and listen to one of his songs and try to copy him.

6. It's nice to be a good singer, but you can get by being just so-so. One form of fun is to try improvised singing—where you make up songs with people on the fly. It sounds very hard but really isn't. The more you sing the more you'll find the world of music enticing.

15

Master the Bench Press

The bench press is the most iconic bodybuilding or strength-training test piece there is. It's the biggest of the big three—the others being the squat and the dead lift. The bench press is the one you see in all the prison movies, where a mistake or a failed burst of power results in the bar crashing into your face or chest. In fact, there is actually a completely safe way to bench-press even without someone "spotting" for you (watching and helping you with the loaded bar).

The bench press starts with you lying on a bench with the loaded bar in a rack behind your head. Your feet touch the ground under the bench. You unrack the weight, lower it to your chest, and, in a powerful explosion of effort, lift it till your arms are straight with locked elbows. You may do several reps before reracking the bar.

1. **Even using a spotter you can be fearful of dropping the bar on yourself. Your spotter might not be paying attention all the time—they could make a mistake or slip—or they might not even be fast and strong enough to really help in an emergency. But if you have fear you'll never master the bench press. The entry trick is very simple: get rid of all the fear by using a power rack. This is a solid device with four uprights that support lateral pegs which stop the bar from crushing you if you drop it. A power rack is pretty much the**

safest way to bench-press, safer even than the machines
that keep the weights in a sealed guide.

2. The rub-pat barrier is mercifully low in bench-pressing.
    As long as you start with low weights you can easily lift
    and work through to success quite easily—the only barrier
    being the fact that bench-pressing is a skill requiring
    coordination as well as strength. And it is not simply a
    straight lift: the bar goes up and back slightly (see picture).
    To bring coordination into your lifting from the word go,
    visualize the bench press as a full-body exercise involving
    every part of you from feet to hands. You connect
    everything by sucking your shoulder blades together and
    naturally arching your back on the bench—so that a flat
    hand could fit easily between your back and the bench. You
    shouldn't overarch—just enough to get the feeling of your
    whole body working as one. Mastering this will allow you
    to make real progress.

3. The right tools aid lifting because they help coordination: a thinner bar that feels really secure in your hands, the correctly sized bench, and the right-height rack will all benefit you.

4. The payoff is very simple with bench-pressing: more weight!

5. Again, the nature of bench-pressing is repeatability. You keep going because you can see yourself getting stronger and stronger.

6. Experiment with the height of the rack, using a spotter to lift and lower the weight down to your chest so you haven't already felt the weight's full shocking heaviness. Practice doing very fast explosive lifts with a light bar, even one devoid of weights. Building the speed is part of the skill of it all.

16

Learn "La Marseillaise"

The best way to begin learning a foreign language is to memorize songs. The words stick much better when they have a tune to them. The French national anthem is "La Marseillaise," written by Claude Joseph Rouget de Lisle in 1792, during the French Revolution. It was banned after Napoleon's reign but brought back by popular demand in 1879—and it has remained the country's anthem ever since.

The entry trick to "La Marseillaise" is the movie *Casablanca*. Get the movie and simply join in, or watch that clip on YouTube. All the right passion and pronunciation is there for you to copy. Keep rewinding and copying until you have it by heart.

"LA MARSEILLAISE"

FRENCH	ENGLISH
Allons enfants de la patrie,	Let us go, children of the fatherland,
Le jour de gloire est arrivé.	Our day of glory has arrived.
Contre nous, de la tyrannie,	Against us stands tyranny,
L'étandard sanglant est levé,	The bloody flag is raised,
L'étandard sanglant est levé,	The bloody flag is raised,
Entendez-vous, dans les campagnes	Do you hear in the countryside

Mugir ces féroces soldats?	The roar of these savage soldiers?
Ils viennent jusque dans nos bras	They come right into our arms
Égorger nos fils, nos compagnes.	To cut the throats of our sons, our countrymen.

REFRAIN	CHORUS
Aux armes, citoyens!	To arms, citizens!
Formez vos bataillons,	Form up your battalions,
Marchons, marchons!	Let us march, let us march!
Qu'un sang impur	That their impure blood
Abreuve nos sillons.	Should water our fields.

Amour sacré de la patrie,	Sacred love of the fatherland,
Conduis, soutiens nos bras vengeurs.	Guide and support our vengeful arms.
Liberté, liberté chérie,	Liberty, beloved liberty,
Combats avec tes défenseurs;	Fight with your defenders;
Combats avec tes défenseurs;	Fight with your defenders;
Sous nos drapeaux, que la victoire	Under our flags, so that victory
Accoure à tes mâles accents;	Will rush to your manly strains;
Que tes ennemis expirants	That your dying enemies
Voient ton triomphe et notre gloire!	Should see your triumph and glory!

REFRAIN	CHORUS

17

Do a Soccer *Elastico*

The *elastico*, in the right hands, or rather feet, looks like magic. The master—whom you can view on the net to be amazed—is still Ronaldinho. He makes it look as if the ball is actually glued to his foot. The move is simple, a refinement of the flip-flap where the attacker taps the ball with the outside of the foot one way to suggest moving to the side, and then quickly reverses the tap to swerve in the other direction. The whole effect relies on combining misdirection with skilled ball control. You need to look to the outside and drop your shoulder and upper body with the first tap of the ball in that direction, and then change direction with your feet before moving the upper body to follow. You are essentially exaggerating a move to the outside in the hope of persuading a defender to move that way and commit before you switch and go inside.

1. The *elastico* is all about practice. If you have a smooth concrete area, warm weather, and a wall in front of you so that the ball comes back if it escapes, you have good starting conditions. Though you'll want to perform on grass, like all subtle soccer moves it's easier to learn on a hard smooth surface. Starting with bare feet is a good entry trick to get a real feel for the ball. You want to caress the ball and get used to the feeling of it not escaping your foot. For this you want

to be moving at the same speed as the ball—which means quite slowly at first.

You start by tapping (or pushing, really) the ball low down with the outside of the foot, where the little toe is. You are kind of gathering up the ball at this point, almost cradling it with the outside and top of the foot. You want the ball to look as though it's moving a good distance but you don't want it to escape from you because then you won't be able to get your foot round the other side so that the inside (the big toe side) can move the ball in the other direction. You can practice the feel of how the foot should move by balancing a ball on your bare foot and seeing if you can control it.

2. The rub-pat skill is this: the stronger the misdirection (the further you move the ball), the harder it is to capture it back quickly. The movement of the shoulders and especially the committed look in the direction you are faking to go must be convincing. At the very same time your feet are doing the

opposite—caressing the ball and shifting it in the other direction. You need to be able to move the ball without looking at it. So practice with your eyes closed a few times, and then with your eyes averted. The amount of lean is important—the more you lean to the side you're faking to, the more committed it looks. You can practice this in front of a mirror, if you like, to get the right sort of feeling associated with the move.

3. Use bare feet at first but then a pair of soccer cleats for an artificial surface. The clunkier the footwear, the harder it is to learn the technique. Specialist street soccer shoes can also help. The bigger the ball, the easier it is—start

    with a good, standard size 5 soccer ball. Alternating between different kinds of balls is also good for refining how you make your foot keep in virtual contact with the ball during the move.

4. In order to get an idea of how "good" your *elastico* is before you debut it on the soccer field, train with a cone or plastic bottle as the defender. Mark out chalk marks on the ground for where you change direction. Make them further and further apart while remembering it is the upper body lean and the all-important look in the wrong direction that are

the heart of how the *elastico* works (once you have the technical side running properly).

5. To avoid getting bored, go on an "*elastico* walk" along the beach or through the park. Go as far as you can, doing *elasticos* as you go, and then come back the other way.

6. Experiment with smaller and smaller balls. Doing an *elastico* with a tennis ball is quite a feat. Stand on a wobble board, the kind used in a gym to build core balance and strength, and try to lean with the upper body one way and the feet the other. Now do this on the ground. See how far you can do this and give it a number relative to the amount (1 for a little, 10 for a lot, for example). When you are on the field, see if you can replicate this amount of lean.

18

Build a Superstack of Wood

Stacking wood is necessary for anyone with a wood-burning stove or open fire. Though countries like Norway have deep traditions of wood splitting and stacking, things are more laissez-faire in southern climes. But the fact is, in times of stress and mental strife, you'd be hard-pressed to find anything more satisfying than splitting logs and stacking them neatly. But then you start to fall into another trap—are your logs really drying? Have you done it right? Could it be better?

You see, the thing about log storage is there are a hundred different ways to do it and as many opinions of how it should be done. Take the innocuous subject of storing a split log bark-up or bark-down. This divides all seasoned wood stackers and yet Lars Mytting, author of *Norwegian Wood* (MacLehose Press, 2015)—a book exclusively about chopping, stacking, and drying wood the Scandi way—has stated it actually makes very little difference even in the rare case of snow lying on top of the pile (which you should avoid anyway). Similar arguments rage about whether logs should be covered, stacked against walls, split when green or when dry . . . the only agreement being that wood stacking itself is highly addictive. It leads to buying fancy axes, mauls, and splitting wedges, and hunting through woods for exotic things to burn.

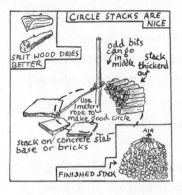

CIRCLE STACKS ARE NICE

SPLIT WOOD DRIES BETTER

odd bits can go in middle

stack thickend out

Use 1 meter rope to make good circle

stack on concrete slab base or bricks

AIR

FINISHED STACK

1. The entry trick is so simple it is beautiful—start by getting a wood moisture meter. The easiest to use have two pins sticking out the top which you insert into the center of the wood or its ends. Recently chopped green wood can be over 50 percent moisture content but you want it down to about 20 percent. A ton of wood at 50 percent moisture content is worth only half the heat value of a ton at 20 percent. With your moisture content meter (good ones are made by Ligno, Dr. Meter, and Stihl and aren't that expensive) you can check exactly how your wood is doing and, what is even more exciting, you can test and experiment with all the different styles of stacking and find out which is really the most effective.

2. Get some decent beech, oak, ash, or thorn—all great firewoods. Pine and spruce produce less heat and are harder to split when green. Oak and beech have small cells so need longer to season—if left as eight-inch (20 cm) diameter, four-foot (1.2 m) logs, they'll need two summers and a winter before they are ready. By splitting and sawing into smaller sizes you can speed up seasoning. Ash and pine have bigger cells and need only spring and summer to season. Split and saw your logs into four and they may be down to 20 percent

moisture content in a single season. Others will tell you that two years are needed. But with your meter you can tell them where to stick their pine logs . . . and, in fact, overseasoned wood loses valuable esters, which actually help burning and increase the calorific value of the wood. Remember, you're burning it, not using it to make a Stradivarius violin.

3. Stacking wood is all about the air and less about keeping it under cover. The better the airflow, the more quickly the inner moisture of the wood, in each cell, evaporates. This is the stuff you want to lose and it's different from water that simply rains down on the stack from the sky. This doesn't penetrate the cells unless there is poor drainage or very shaded and stifling storage conditions. So the key is to stack the wood off the ground on a base of concrete slabs with plenty of gaps for air to circulate. To immediately gain superstacker status go for a circular "shaker-style" wood stack. This looks fancy and works very well but is easy to build. On top of your concrete slabs (you only need a few to keep the bottom logs off the wet ground) make a circle of logs like spokes of a wheel with the thinner ends in the middle. Leave an empty circle in the center—this is for air circulation—though some use it for storing more logs. Gradually build up the circle avoiding "runs"—where a natural line of logs open up a vertical gap—this will collapse when you start depleting the pile. Leave the logs bare on top or cover with planks, but leave the center open to increase airflow.

4. Splitting wood is best done using a proper ax with a fat head. Otherwise it is very satisfying to use wedges and a sledge hammer. Splitting your own wood and then stacking it well will increase your knowledge of woodcraft matters greatly. People admire stacked wood and draw conclusions about your character—let them. Offer to test their wood with your meter and become a stacking expert.

5. Every year you'll have to stack wood—plenty of chances to get better. Increase the gameability by making different kinds of stack. Experiment with these stacks of wood and use the meter to decide which is best. Whether you cover the wood or not depends largely on rainfall and prevailing winds. You may find that it makes little difference where you live.

19

Develop Film Using Coffee and Salt

Old cameras are fun but it's expensive to send off the film to be developed. Buying the right chemicals is less pricey but a bit complicated. However, neither are necessary—very decent photographs can be obtained by developing film in instant coffee! You don't even need Nescafé Gold Blend; supermarket standard issue works fine. You'll also need some washing soda and some kitchen salt to fix the results. If you add vitamin C you can speed up the process but it's not essential. You can use old expired films— black-and-white or color—the results using either have a cool brownish-sepia tinge.

You don't need any special gear—not even a developing tank— all you need is pitch darkness—so wait until night or do this in a cellar.

Lots of people who have only used digital cameras are keen to learn about film and processing it. Using caffenol—the active ingredient in the instant coffee/soda mix used—is a good way to learn the real basics of how film works. It's a way to connect to the very early history of film when ordinary substances—such as salt and even eggs—were used in the process. You can cut up film into different pieces and experiment by developing them in different brands of coffee or for different lengths of time. Flickr, the photo-sharing website, has vast numbers of caffenol-developed pictures you can be inspired by.

1. Get an old film, or a new one, and run it through a camera—35mm is easiest to find but 120 film is also available and easier to handle as it is shorter. You'll need a bottle opener to pry open the film canister. This must be done in pitch darkness. You then unspool the film into a small bucket or jug. If you choose to use 120 film the negatives are bigger and you'll get twelve on a roll rather than thirty-six. You unroll the film and strip off the backing paper before dumping it in the bucket.

2. Add 3 teaspoons of washing soda (Arm & Hammer is a standard brand) to 125 ml of tap water at around 70°F. Add 6 teaspoons of instant coffee to another 125 ml, then mix the two solutions and add another 100 ml of water. Depending on the size of your bucket increase the ingredients proportionately to cover the film. This is your basic developing mix. It brings out the picture, but if you turn the lights on the image will fade instantly. (We'll cover fixing it shortly.) Wear thin rubber gloves and add the film to the mix, stirring all the time with chopsticks or something similar. The idea is to keep the film from sticking to itself and not getting developed. However, cool patterns can happen even if this does occur. Bear in mind that washing soda is harmful if swallowed.

3. Keep stirring for twenty-five minutes. If you want to make it work faster, add some vitamin C.

4. Pour out the mixture and put the film under three rinses of plain water. If you want weird black dots, then rinse it in a mixture of vinegar and water instead.

5. Now add 350 g of salt to a liter of water warmed to 95°F. This is the fixer that makes the picture remain visible when you turn the lights on. You might need a blender to speed up the dissolving. If a few grains remain, ignore them. However, the solution must be supersaturated to work; in other words, you have to heat and stir the water until almost all the salt is dissolved.

6. Dump the salt fixer over the film and leave for several hours. If the temperature is around 70°F leave for twenty-four hours to be on the safe side. At 95°F it can be fixed in three hours.

Wash the film for five minutes under the tap, then hang it up to dry—magic! You can easily scan the negatives in and either print them or post them online. There are plenty of ways to turn negatives into positives—Photoshop Elements (the budget version of Photoshop) is one of several options easily downloaded.

20

Do a High-Speed Getaway J-Turn

You've seen it in the movies a hundred times, or, if you're old enough, in 1970s TV series such as *The Rockford Files*. The bad guys appear in front, usually firing out of the windows of their black Cadillacs or Mercs. The good guys reverse at high speed, do something clever, and then the car spins round 180 degrees, now pointing in the right direction. They roar off after the rear windshield has been shattered into a thousand shards without a single bullet hitting either of the passengers. This is the so called J-turn and, unlike the slightly trickier hand-brake turn, it is actually quite easy to learn.

1. **The entry trick is all about the car. In a manual car with ABS brakes you'll need to double declutch—which means pressing the clutch down, putting the car in neutral and releasing the clutch, and then pressing the clutch again to engage first gear after the turn—all a bit complicated to do in a fraction of a second. If your manual car has no ABS you'll still have to change gear. BUT if you have an ordinary automatic—front- or rear-wheel drive, ABS or not—you're set up for making fabulous J-turns after only a little bit of practice.**

Reverse the above in a right-hand-drive car

2. The right car needs the right place to practice. A parking lot with a loose surface will work but still take its toll on the tires. A wet and greasy piece of tarmac is good, but probably easiest is a damp, flat piece of field.

3. The move starts with a high-speed reverse. Get up to 20–25mph—which will mean the engine will be making a nice screaming whine. Hold the steering wheel with one hand low down and one higher up (or one-handed, as in the drawing, if you are feeling confident). At the point of the turn, suddenly slack off the acceleration but don't touch the brake. This throws the weight of the car forward and off the front wheels. Then you flick the steering wheel round, pushing up with the lower hand and down with the upper hand. The front will fly round. At the point where you are now facing the opposite direction apply a quick overturn to steady the car in the right direction. At that point jam the gear stick into DRIVE and roar forward. The whole trick is in timing the move so that you go forward and don't spin more

Halfway through the 180° SPIN...

Ram it into DRIVE...

As the SPIN finishes go back to '12 o'clock' + accelerate...

FOOT ON THE GAS

than 180 degrees, or turn too slowly and not make it spin enough. You need to practice and get a feel for the weight of the car slumping forward as you smartly take your foot off the gas. That weight transfer is better in a lower car, as SUVs can wobble a bit or even roll.

4. The J-turn is taught at tactical driving schools to would-be bodyguards as a method of escape and evasion, but its use for the ordinary driver is building a feel for how weight affects steering. Once you know how to J-turn a car you'll have a pretty good feel for how far you can push it before it leaves the road. And by training on grassy fields you'll learn a lot about the way skids start and stop.

21

Make Sushi . . . That Actually Looks and Tastes Like Sushi

Sushi is just a piece of fish on top of a lump of rice. It should be so easy and yet it isn't. But if you can make real sushi you'll have made something everyone wants to try—because even having it in a restaurant is no guarantee it'll be good.

1. **The trick is: even though you think it's the topping that counts, really, it's all in the rice. A sushi chef in Japan will concur that good sushi is 30 percent filling and 70 percent rice, but for the purposes of people brought up on Western ways of making rice it should be more like 85 percent rice, 15 percent filling. Once you have the rice right everything else follows quite easily.**

2. **Easily, if you have sushi-grade fish and a very sharp knife, that is. But back to the rice. Get the very best—which means the most expensive usually—Japanese rice you can find. It has to be short grain and from a Japanese manufacturer. The best type is known as *uruchimai*, and the best version of that is *koshihikari*, which is grown only in Japan, Australia, and the U.S. You want *shinmai*, or this year's crop. Nothing else will work anywhere near as well. The reason is that rice less than a year old requires one cup of water to each cup of rice. Older rice will be drier and need more water, which makes it**

harder to cook exactly right. With the right rice you're off to a great start. It needs to be washed in ten changes of cold water before you use it—this way it'll be rid of the starches that accumulate around it. If you don't wash the rice this thoroughly it'll be far too glutinous and sticky. You want grains that stick together and coalesce into a single unit but still retain a certain dryness (without being dry of course). You can make the rice in a rice cooker or a pot—but a rice cooker is better. Immediately after cooking, mix it with the salt, sugar, rice vinegar, and rice wine that helps give the rice its characteristic flavor. Use four cups of rice to a cup of unseasoned rice vinegar, a teaspoon of salt, half a cup of sugar, and a quarter-cup of rice wine as a starting point. A good brand of rice vinegar is Marukan unseasoned (seasoned vinegar already has salt and sugar in it). The sugary version of rice wine called Mirin can be used instead of adding sugar at the end.

3. You need to cool the rice before using it—get a fan and sift through the grains as you mix in your Japanese rice vinegar flavoring. This has the added impact of giving it that slight sheen you want in good sushi rice. The rice should be about room temperature before you start to use it. Generally, the longer you leave it the easier it will become to mold—half a day is good—but leave it too long and the sheen will have left the rice and it will have started to dry out. When molding into sushi, use about a middle finger's width and a little finger's length of rice for classic nigiri sushi, where the fish sits on top of the rice, and a little-finger's width for

roll-type maki sushi. The secret is not to squeeze the rice into shape but to slap it between your palms. You want it to stick together but you don't want the air squeezed out of it. It's easier if you wear thin, see-through plastic gloves to stop the rice sticking to your hands.

4. Experiment with how much rice wine and vinegar to use and how long you leave the rice and how much you cool it. The fan is a better cooler than the fridge, which doesn't dry it out as effectively. And sushi was invented long before ice boxes and freezers.

5. Now the easy bit is either adding the filling (for maki) or the top (for nigiri). Buy fish that the fishmonger guarantees is good to eat raw. If you can get mackerel that has just been caught, it makes great sushi. In all cases, whether it is tuna, salmon, or mackerel, use the sharpest knife you can find to slice it up. The look of sushi with its fine-cut edges is as important, almost, as the flavor and certainly contributes to the experience. Having molded a finger-width slab of rice, lay the fish on top and eat—using soy sauce and wasabi to add to the flavor and aid digestion.

22

Tell a Story That Will Enthrall Any Child

It isn't usually until you have kids that your ability to make up stories comes into question, and it can be scary. You may find you just can't come up with the goods, however creative you think you are. What you need is the unlimited storymaking power that we all have lurking inside us; releasing that power requires some inhibitory processes to be turned off.

1. **The entry trick: stories are about reusing stuff that comes beforehand. If you start with a good platform—that is a starting situation with material ripe for multiple use, such as magic items, wizards, heroes, naughty boys and girls—then you are off easily.**

2. **The best stories are full of drama, and drama is NOT about conflict. When you start trying to tell stories you may inadvertently be led down this blind alley. Instead, you need to think about submission and domination. It isn't the fight that interests, it's how some give in and others win that is interesting. So think about people who dominate others— bosses, tyrants, teachers—and think about reversals— underdogs, bad servants, naughty kids. The master–servant dynamic is good. As is the teacher–student—think Gandalf and Bilbo, Harry Potter and Severus Snape. My best story series was about two identical twins who were very, very**

naughty. That ran for lots of nights. Another great one is a time-travel machine that takes you back to interesting periods in history. Another they liked was the incredible shrinking machine—a great way to reuse everything.

3. The rub-pat barrier is simple—we want to solve problems as humans and we are good at it. But a story is about piling problems and difficulties on. You need to get a different, sadistic head on. You also need to look backward, not forward, as you tell stories. Keep bringing stuff in that has been mentioned. If nothing comes to you to move the story on, reuse material until something does come to you. Incidentally, this is the correct way to think about it: don't consciously "think stuff up"—wait for it to come to you.

4. The payoff is gratitude and a boost in self-worth as a parent.

5. Every night you get to try something new. If you're really keen you might even make a list of good ideas before you enter their bedroom. But it's better just to let ideas come to you in the darkness. I've found that stories are very dependent on promising platforms—so if you start with a bad one then reel it in fast and get a new one with more potential contradictions and drama built in—which means more disparities in status. If you have a superhero and a worm you have a story . . .

23

Immobilize Someone with an Aikido Hold

Aikido is the ancient and previously secret Japanese martial art of locks and throws. A fiendish knowledge of the way the body's joints lock together is exploited to immobilize an opponent. The idea of using the opponent's strength against them is utilized in aikido, though there are several other equally important principles to the art. And all of them are present in *nikajo*, or *nikyo*, as it is sometimes called. This is the simplest form of wrist lock that also immobilizes the shoulder and the elbow, bringing the attacker down to their knees whimpering for mercy . . .

In Steven Seagal's *Under Siege 2* a version of *nikajo* is taught by the hulking brute himself. The basic form is set up by asking your "attacker" to hold you by the opposite wrist to his. You then wrap your fingers around his so he can't let go. Once you have trapped his fingers, you bring the other hand down in cutting fashion over the wrist, making the attacker fall to the ground.

1. **The entry trick is all about thinking of the wrist, elbow, and shoulder as a triangle in the same plane. If you can level all these three into a triangle you can then imagine whaling down on that triangle and as all three joints are locked together the whole body has no choice but to drop to its knees. Your power comes not from your wrists—they simply deliver power and control its delivery. The actual power that drops your opponent comes from the knees.**

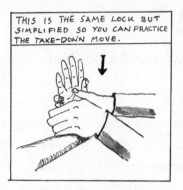

THIS IS THE SAME LOCK BUT SIMPLIFIED SO YOU CAN PRACTICE THE TAKE-DOWN MOVE.

WRIST GRABS WRIST, YOU TRAP OPPONENT'S HAND SO HE CAN'T LET GO.

THEN DROP YOUR WEIGHT

2. Work with someone who isn't scared of you and preferably has reasonably robust arms. Not that you can hurt someone unless you really try in *nikajo*, it's just that they will be more relaxed, and that makes it a lot easier to learn.

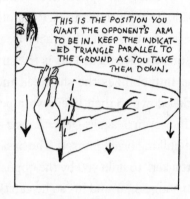

THIS IS THE POSITION YOU WANT THE OPPONENT'S ARM TO BE IN. KEEP THE INDICAT--ED TRIANGLE PARALLEL TO THE GROUND AS YOU TAKE THEM DOWN.

3. The rub-pat barrier is subtle. You have to try and make real that visualization of the triangle linking the shoulder, elbow, and wrist. Then you have to try and steer into it while controlling their wrist. You will start to get a feel for the lock and the temptation will be to apply power through the arms. You need some power from here but it is more about power delivery. You need to think of the weight you have dropping when your knees flex, and that travels down your arms to control your opponent. Knee power is felt as something far

stronger than mere upper-body strength, even if it is a monster crushing your wrists. You have to imagine sort of sucking the person in and down, and if they can be on the brink of overbalancing forward it is easier.

4. *Nikajo* is a good party trick. You do it on someone. They do it on you. Since you are trying to make it "work" rather than merely showing off, you need some cooperation from the partner. They offer resistance but sensible resistance—they aren't trying to kick you in the nuts as you set up the move. Remember, this is the stylized form of the lock—in a fight you may only use a fragmentary version of it. But the lock helps build all kinds of useful body awareness.

5. All sorts of experimentation are needed with *nikajo*. Try moving backward and forward with your partner. Try keeping the elbows in and then out. Give numbers to how much wrist and knee strength you apply. All this builds awareness of how the body works. Most importantly, it builds awareness of how interconnected the parts of the body are. It is knowledge of this interconnectedness that aikido exploits.

24

Juggle Four Balls

Juggling is a great skill, beloved of the genius and polymathic computer scientist Claude Shannon. Studies have shown that juggling actually builds measurable connections in the brain, so it really is a good mind/body workout. While many can juggle three balls, it isn't really that much more difficult to juggle four. What's more, it can be broken down more easily as each hand is independent of the other, allowing you to practice both separately.

1. The entry trick is keeping your eyes fixed on a point above eye level, or even at eye level, as long as it is beyond the balls' trajectory, so start by practicing opposite something obvious at that height, such as a picture on the wall. With your eyes anchored in the middle distance your peripheral vision monitors all the activity at the top of the balls' trajectory—this is what you need to be aware of, not the basic reaction of catching the balls. If you keep your eyes watching the balls at the top of their curve you will automatically adjust to catching them. To start, simply practice throwing one ball up and down, throwing and catching from one hand, keeping the eyes fixed ahead. When throwing, do small circular "dips" before you throw. You can dip to the outside or the inside as long as the ball describes an arc. You can also dip along a center line so the arc extends away from you rather than from side to side.

Now attempt to throw and catch two balls in each hand. While one is in the air, at the top of its trajectory, release the second. When it is at its top you should be able to throw the one you caught. Both hands do the same thing, cycling two balls.

LOOK WHERE YOU WANT THE BALLS TO GO. NOT AT YOUR HANDS.

Juggling 2 balls in each hand 4 balls is really

Make small circles as you throw

2. The rub-pat barrier is getting over the urge to wait for a ball to come to hand before launching another. You need to switch from focusing on individual processes to a unified and circular motion of catching and throwing. With your eyes fixed on the middle distance you will feel you have more time to throw and catch. You start learning to do this by holding three or four balls in one hand and throwing each one ONLY when the previous one hits the top point of the trajectory. You then catch all of them in sequence in the other hand. Then start again. This builds the awareness to move to the next stage, throwing and catching two balls in one hand. Then move to doing the other hand and finally both hands at once.

3. Start with hacky-sack-type balls. They don't bounce and they are easy to catch. Practice over a large table or your bed—that way when you drop the balls you don't have to bend down all the time.

4. Juggling is a great thing to teach others. People will get very quickly bored of watching you juggle but will spend hours patiently trying to learn themselves.

5. Carry two hacky sack balls with you all the time and practice whenever you get a chance and have something to fix your middle-distance vision on.

6. Experiment with scarves, blunt knives, fruit—including bananas. Often longer objects are easier to catch and throw.

25

Master the Three-Card Trick

An old friend who has a first-class degree from Oxford University in logic, math, and philosophy lost $100 on the streets of New York to this trick. It's one of the oldest in the book and yet there's always some sucker out there who thinks he's cleverer than everyone else. The trick is only the cornerstone of the con—which involves having fake betters bet and lose on the game until you are forced to come in believing you are the *only* one who can see where the real card (usually the ace of spades) is. Of course, you win once and then it's double or quit . . .

The three-card trick is also a genuine piece of sleight of hand. You hear a lot about this when you want to learn magic but many of the first tricks you learn don't really require it, or are basic moves rather than finished tricks. The three-card monte, as it is also known, is a perfect magic micromastery as it involves both sleight of hand and patter and has an astonishing effect.

1. **The entry trick—well, it's a trick, so there has to be one— revolves around being able to throw cards down that are stacked in one hand. To make this easier, arch or bend the cards lengthwise so they sit on the table with their long edges down but the middle a bit off the top. This bend shouldn't be noticeable to the betters but it will help you grip and throw the cards. Next, when you are holding two cards in one hand you need to be able to throw either the**

top or the bottom one down without anyone noticing the difference. So when you throw the top card—which you show—down, you do it naturally. When you throw the bottom card from beneath it you need to switch the holding fingers at the moment of card release, so that the fingers that were holding the bottom card move up to the top card. So if a thumb and two fingers were holding the two cards, with two fingers on the bottom card, there are still two on the "bottom" card. Practicing this move is the key to the whole thing.

2. The rub-pat barrier will take a few hours of practice to conquer—but you will manage it fairly easily. Practice in front of a mirror as this will also aid your ability to do the right patter. Mirrors seem to have the effect of prompting monologues.

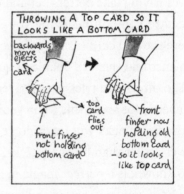

THROWING A TOP CARD SO IT LOOKS LIKE A BOTTOM CARD

backwards move ejects card

top card flies out

front finger not holding bottom card

front finger now holding old bottom card — so it looks like top card

You need to coordinate the throwdown with the finger switch. The throwdown uses the thumb and forefinger to release the card as if you are throwing the top one down. But you hold it in place with the next two fingers. At the same time you release the bottom card and allow the snap motion of throwing to eject it out from underneath. You then move up the lower fingers to the top card to make it look like it is the bottom card. Making that move up at the same time as you extend the "throwing" thumb and forefinger is the secret. The throw attracts attention away from the finger move. Taken all together it looks like the top card went down.

3. The cards you use can make it easier to learn—plastic coated cards don't stick together and are easier to handle with sweaty paws. A constant pattern on the back rather than one which alters is harder to monitor and easier to trick people with. If someone gets eye level with the table spin a card out to hit them in the eye but don't do the trick. It relies on having a topside angle of perception. Fortunately, there is another variant you can use where you swap the position of the cards higher up. But if someone wants to eyeball the pack they haven't swallowed the con—they've assumed there is a trick so it is best to not try it with them.

4. So, bolting that into the three-card trick, you first gather an audience. You hold up the three cards—a jack in one hand and a jack and an ace in the other. The ace is on top of the jack. You tap it to further direct their attention to it. You then throw the cards down normally and switch them around—slowly at first. You turn over the ace to confirm where it is. The audience secretly congratulates itself on following the switch. Then you speed up the switching and get the audience to imagine it is this that causes them to lose sight of it. Either that, or you picking it up and swapping it during the switching.

5. Keep going until you sense they are getting cocky. That's when you do the switch and catch them out. Then do a few more normal ones. When the money is laid on the card, do the switch again.

6. There are lots of ways to experiment. You can hold up the two cards—ace behind jack and make as if to throw down the jack. You then show there is still a jack in your hand (they assume you had both jacks to start with). But then you show that the ace is on the table. You can bend up a corner of one card to show them that is the card they are following but secretly take out the bend as you hold the cards in your hand, using the same switch to send out a bottom rather than a top card. And lastly, even if you know the trick, never bet on it . . .

26

Grow a Bonsai Tree

Mr. Miyagi, the inscrutable master in the movie *The Karate Kid*, was a bonsai master as well as a fearsome fighting machine. Somehow bonsai treemanship is viewed as difficult and arcane, but in fact it isn't that tricky to achieve good results in a few growing seasons.

1. **Use a fast-growing willow, a medium-speed maple, a slower oak, and a very slow-growing pine. Having only one bonsai is dispiriting. Having several means you can switch from one to another and learn from faster plants.**

2. **Buy good pruning clippers that are satisfying to use, pots you enjoy the sight of, and, of course, trees. Get your trees from a nursery, or from the wild if you have access to small saplings. You can even get good trees at supermarkets for a few pounds. This is your basic starting plant, which you will prune mainly on the top to redistribute the growth lower down and achieve the bonsai effect.**

3. **What makes a bonsai look like a miniature tree? Having a tapered trunk and very small buttress-type roots. You just don't see these things in nature except in miniature pines up near the mountain snow line. So the rub-pat barrier is: How do you make a tapered trunk without making the tree tall? The answer is: The more you prune, the slower the growth of**

the trunk. And the smaller the pot, the slower the growth. The Japanese have devised several techniques to create the effect of a tapered trunk. One of the quicker methods is to start with a tree that is actually quite tall—such as a sapling from a nursery. Then

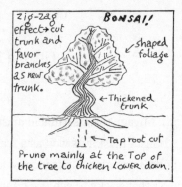

cut it off very low and wait for it to sprout. You then cut back all the sprouts except the most promising, which you train upward with a twist of copper wire (removed before it cuts in). This is repeated as the tree grows upward.

To make the roots grow in a decorative way, remove the tap root (the obvious big root whose function is to keep the tree upright—it's not needed in a pot) and carefully prune the other roots to make a root ball rather than individual long roots. The root ball will force roots to the surface, which looks good. However, the roots store food so you can supplement the plant with extra fertilizer to stimulate growth.

Making smaller leaves is another trade-off with growth as the leaves are what create growth energy. If you cut leaves in summer they will grow back—but smaller. This is one way to further the illusion of a miniature tree.

But the biggest error is to overprune your bonsai. It is better to let it grow for several weeks at a time without pruning to let it become strong. Then in late winter, when the plant is dormant, cut it back very strongly to a shape even less than that which is desired. It will then grow back and make up the difference.

4. As suggested, most bonsai growers have many trees on the go at once. These are of different varieties that grow at different rates, allowing for experimentation and greater decorative effect. Wiring branches (so they bend upward sooner than usual) and even squeezing the trunk with carefully applied pieces of copper plate (this can be used to thicken it lower down) are all ways to make the tree grow the way you want it to.

27

Make a Perfect Soufflé Every Time

If the omelet is the test piece of the home cook, the soufflé is the examination decider for the would-be professional. And many pros can't make a good one, least of all every time. But cooking is more about calibrating and practicing than about hype, so why not start with a soufflé today? It's a great micromastery to have under your belt and always impresses. The basic form of soufflé uses a béchamel sauce—butter and flour—but you can always move on to more exotic ingredients. The engine of the soufflé remains the same, though—egg whites and sauce, beaten to provide a barrier against escaping air, steam, and gas that has been trapped in bubbles inside the egg whites. This causes the hardened crust to rise like a cork popping from a bottle. Hopefully.

The first thing is to make the béchamel sauce, which coats the egg whites and provides something to push against (and taste). Use 100 g of butter and 100 g of sifted flour to make the sauce. Add warm milk rather than cold milk to make it smoother. Then use 7 egg whites to make the rising mix. Keep them separate for the time being.

1. **The entry tricks to soufflé making are various—but at first it's best to apply all of them to give yourself the best chance of success. To make the bubble cells in the egg whites stronger add a little acid to the mix—half a teaspoon of cream of tartar. When beating the eggs only do so until they**

begin to really stiffen. Don't overbeat them to oblivion—they need to be just resistant to movement when you tilt the bowl on its side (not tip it upside down).

2. The best whites are from room-temperature fresh eggs. Cold eggs inhibit the ability of the mix to set without excessive beating. Make sure there is no yolk in the white: it makes it harder to beat. Use a wire beater attachment to get more air in. Proper soufflé dishes will make you feel more professional. Make sure the oven temperature really is 395°F and use the bottom shelf. It certainly helps if you can look in and see what is happening without opening the door.

3. The rub-pat barrier is all in maintaining the integrity of the bubbles. This needs to be done to get it to rise. On the other hand, you have to mix the whites and béchamel sauce properly to get it to taste nice. If you mix it together too well or too fiercely, then the bubbles will disintegrate, so you use a sort of sliding-in technique—do it piece by piece, not all at once in a big slop—to fold the egg white mix into the béchamel. It's better that there are still a few stripes of white visible in the mix than something completely beaten to a pulp.

4. Once the mix is made, tip it into butter-greased soufflé dishes. Run your palette knife over the top and rim the inside with your finger to get a professional top-hat look when it rises. Now quickly cook the tops of the soufflés under a hot grill for a minute or two (or carefully use a blow

torch). This will make the crust stronger and more likely to rise well. Then put them in the bottom of the oven and cook for 12 minutes, watching all the time. Most soufflés are ruined by cooks taking their eye off the ball to attend to some other task. No! When you are making soufflés, that is all you are doing.

5. Make sweet and savory soufflés to practice. No one will turn them down. Experiment with coating the inside of the ramekin with bread crumbs or sugar as this can help the mixture to rise higher.

28

Make a Perfect Cube of Wood

You want to get into woodwork, or simply learn to use woodworking tools—but where to start? I asked Petter Southall—a highly skilled Norwegian-American cabinet maker—what the micromastery for this would be, and he answered without hesitation, "Make a cube of wood. If you can make a perfect cube of wood you have all the skills you need for any kind of woodwork."

The sting in the tail is: it sounds easier than it is. Making a rough cube is very easy—get a length of square section timber and measure off enough to make a cuboid shape, make a cut using a saw, and there is your cube. But it will be far from perfect. The problems start when you use the plane and saw to adjust the flatness of each surface—and, of course, they all affect each other. The analogy is the old problem of lowering a chair. You cut a bit off each leg, but it is uneven, so you cut a bit more off one, and then another, and finally the chair has no legs at all.

You can take on this challenge using power tools or you can use hand tools. I think it's better and more skillful to use hand tools, so we'll assume you're doing that.

1.   **The best way to approach the challenge is to first experience how difficult it is. Get a piece of standard square section timber (2 in or 2.5 in square is common) and saw off, say, a 2.25 in length. This basic cube should be checked with a set square and an accurate ruler. Shade the areas of wood that**

don't fit and plane them off. With care, cut the cube down to its correct length.

This is where accurate sawing comes in—done well, it can produce a cube requiring very little or even no planing and sanding at all.

This is the entry trick—sawing accurately with a Japanese saw. The Japanese saw cuts on the pull stroke, not the push stroke as Western saws do. Consequently the blade can be much thinner and sharper. A fine Japanese saw can cut like a knife and the width of the cut will be much narrower than that made by a normal carpentry saw. This narrow cut means much greater precision is possible. The surface is much cleaner—a cross-grain cut by a Japanese saw will look shiny, as if it has been planed rather than sawn. The Japanese specialize in making very fancy interlocking joints—using a Western saw it isn't easy to make such joints, and a lot of cleaning up with a chisel is needed. But if you measure accurately the Japanese saw may make the only cut you need.

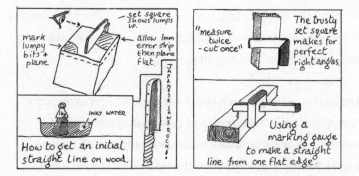

2. Okay, so you've made your first almost-perfect cube by sawing off ready-planed wood. Now you need to start from scratch for the real challenge—in other words, get a piece of tree and go from there. Roughly saw the wood into a squarish shape. The rub-pat barrier is this: the more you cut off one side the more you will have to cut off another side to make it match up. The way to reduce this is to take your uneven lump of wood (it's cheating to start with ready-planed wood) and immerse it in a bath of inky water. The tidemark line will be perfectly level. Try to get it so that the grain is either perpendicular to the water or in line with it. This will make planing easier. Now cut along the line with extreme care using the saw. You can then use a marking gauge to cut a flat surface opposite it—leaving you with a flat plank of wood. You can verify how flat it is using a set square. Gaps of light showing under the set square's straight metal edge will need to be planed off. Identify these raised areas and shade them in with pencil. Then remove the shading with a properly adjusted plane. The plank may end up thinner but it will be perfectly flat and both sides will be parallel.

3. Now to make a square-sectioned length. Using a set square and steel point (to make a thin, precise line for the saw) draw lines at each end that are square with the surfaces of the plank. If your sawing has a margin of error, leave 1/16 in to plane it flat later. Do this for all edges if you have yet to master perfect sawing. When the ends are square, you can rule parallel lines down the plank to make the square section.

4. This is a major achievement—next step is cutting off a cube. This is where it gets tricky—and if your sawing is off, trying to fix it with a plane will probably mess the whole thing up. The trick is to get one end perfectly square with all four sides of the bar then draw an encircling line around the other end as accurately as you can. Once you have sawn this you should have a near-perfect cube. Use the set square to identify lumpy bits, which you shade and remove using a plane.

5. The key is to make lots of cubes—make a set of wooden blocks for a toddler. Try to learn on each cube just how much leeway you need to give to be able to perfect the cube with the plane. Become sensitive to the width of the saw cut and how much it distorts the final shape. Learning to make allowances for this is a big part of success.

6. Try using a powered circular saw to see how much easier it is. You can set the width very accurately and all cuts will be 100 percent square. Look in books for other traditional ways to make a cube—what I've shown is only one of many. The skills you develop will enable you to make joints quite easily, and once you can join wood together in a functional and decorative manner, you are well on your way to being able to make anything.

29

Mix a Delightful Daiquiri

It is said that the key cocktail, in which all the elements and secrets of cocktail making are present in some form or another, is the daiquiri. In it are combined a base alcohol, sourness in the form of lime juice, and sweetness in sugar. A cocktail is a balancing act between these three. The great master of cocktail making, David Embury, divided cocktails into "aromatics" and "sours"—the key aromatic being the dry martini where vermouth is mixed with gin. There is a case for saying bitterness is needed when sourness is not in proliferation, hence the need for quinine in a gin and tonic—a gin and soda just isn't the same. But in a daiquiri sourness is there in profusion in the form of lime juice, so there is no need to add further balancing elements of bitterness.

The daiquiri is an American refinement of an age-old South American drink found from Brazil to Cuba—cane alcohol, sugar, limes, and ice. In various forms you can drink this anywhere. But in the small town of Daiquiri in Cuba after the 1898 Spanish–American War was fought in that country, American engineer Jennings Cox wrote down and perfected the daiquiri recipe. Most importantly, he noted the importance of crushed ice to chill the drink fast.

The pronunciation can provide a slight initial problem—though it is often pronounced "dackery," the correct way is "dykery." More importantly, it's a deceptively simple cocktail that involves eight parts of white Cuban rum to two parts of lime juice to one part of sugar syrup. These are considered the classic proportions though, of course, they can be experimented with. Most cocktails follow this 8:2:1 formula—a daiquiri could be seen as a whiskey sour that simply substitutes rum and lime for the whiskey and lemon.

1. The trick is to use frozen equipment; this reduces the amount of dilution to a controllable amount. Start with cool rum and cooled juice from the fridge and use ice cubes and a cocktail shaker that has been in the freezer. Unlike aromatics, which benefit from stirring and not shaking, the daiquiri needs a good shake and the ice cubes need to be finely crushed.

2. The best ingredients make the best cocktails. The daiquiri needs a light rum and the best is anything that approaches Bacardi Carta Blanca. Lime juice should be freshly squeezed and cooled. You can use sugar but it doesn't dissolve well in cold rum. Better to make sugar syrup from a cup of hot water and two cups of superfine sugar. This can be kept refrigerated for months.

3. The rub-pat barrier with the daiquiri, as with all cocktails, lies in controlling the amount of dilution. You need some, but too much destroys the drink. Too little and the ingredients don't blend together into a seamless whole. While some blend the ice and rum in a blender, you have to be careful the pulverized ice doesn't make the rum too wet and weak. Traditionally, an ice-cold shaker is filled with the rum, the lime juice, the sugar syrup, and the crushed ice. This

is shaken vigorously. Obviously, if all the ingredients are ice-cold, you can shake it longer without excess dilution occurring. You then pour the mix through a strainer and serve. (The raw form of the drink keeps the crushed ice in—but that will become watery by the time you finish.)

4. Cocktails need parties—and these are a great way to refine your abilities. Alter the temperature of the ingredients, the amount you crush the ice, and how much lime peel you include with the lime (the peel is bitter and some say none should be allowed to taint a daiquiri, while more youthful palettes beg to differ).

5. The competitive cocktail party involves four or five daiquiri "stations"—each one made in a slightly different way. Each station starts with the same amount of ingredients. Whoever runs out first—the most popular—is the winner. The winner's basic recipe is used as the starting point for the next party—over several parties you should arrive at a perfect result . . .

30

Walk the Tango Walk

A tango is a tango is a tango—but a tango walk is something special. It is in the downtime from the fancy well-known tango flourishes that a true tango spirit is known. There is nothing easier to spot in a novice than a tango walk that lacks conviction. It is in the walking parts of the tango that you need to give your best, and when your tango walk is good, your tango will be excellent. And the reason for all this is that actually tango in its basic form is simply walking with someone. There are no set moves—you just let the rhythm capture you and your partner's spirit as you walk back and forth.

But the word "walk" gives people the wrong idea. A tango walk means moving with attitude, balance, and rhythm.

1. **The entry trick is this—shift your center to your genitals. Most people have their center quite high—in their heads or upper chest. That's why they overbalance easily. But if you shift your balance lower—to the pelvic genital region—you'll be much more stable. Also, a strange thing happens: you engage a different part of the brain—the part that worries less and moves more surefootedly. The trick is to bend the knees very slightly. Then put your chest forward so that it is over the knee. You'll be teetering on your toes now and will want to make a walking motion forward, which is the basic**

start of a tango walk. Now if you shift one foot back a little to balance, you can focus on lowering your center to the pelvic region. Imagine your eyes have shifted and are seeing out from somewhere in your lower belly. That's right, your worldview is now at waist height. With this in mind, you are ready to start a great tango walk.

2. Tango walking can be practiced anywhere—even, in slightly tamed form, in the street. You don't need special gear—but light, well-fitting shoes help. At the start, loose clothing helps too. When you are walking tango-style, your image should be of a careful cat or other wild creature, utterly balanced and testing each step as it goes. You "arm" each step by bending the back knee and being ready to move—this is why you never overbalance. You then snake out the front foot—toe first, even if your heel strikes first: it doesn't really matter as long as you roll each foot and caress the floor like a cat walking.

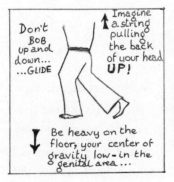

Don't BOB up and down... ...GLIDE

Imagine a string pulling the back of your head UP!

Be heavy on the floor, your center of gravity low - in the genital area...

Tango walking is much easier when you LEAN before mak--ing a STEP

Wear clothes that make you feel SEXY

3. To initiate a step, overbalance by getting your chest in line with your knee. Now imagine that your upper body is just sitting on your lower body—which is doing all the work. Your hips aren't going up and down and neither is your head, as it does in normal walking; instead you are shifting horizontally, almost, and your knees are taking in the up-and-down movement. The rub-pat barrier is holding this all together in rhythm when you are also moving forward. The way around this is to think of dragging your back toe a little along the floor as you make each forward step. This builds in the rhythm to each step and gives a sense of start and finish to each one. You stay low while you walk. Your nose should not be going up and down in a "V" fashion as it does in normal walking. If it moves up and down, it should be more of a smooth "U" shape.

4. The walk is all about letting the body do the thinking. The idea is that the right walk liberates your dancing instincts, which combine with those of your partner. Like sex, really, as all tango fans will tell you.

31

Make Fire by Rubbing Two Sticks Together

You might well have seen survival experts on TV making fire by using a bow drill, but a much rarer sight is the purer form of rubbing two sticks together—the hand drill. A simple, thin, straight stick of elder or some other wood with a pith interior is rotated in a baseboard made of clematis or willow wood (for best results). As it begins to smoke, you cut a notch connecting the blackened circle to the edge of the baseboard. This notch is where the black smoking dust congregates and hopefully forms a dull glowing coal. The coal is then transferred to a ball of tinder (typically inner-bark fibers rubbed as fine as hair) and wafted in the air to catch fire.

Rich Lisney, founder of the outdoor magazine *The Bimbler* and expert hand-driller, gave me some tips on how to micromaster this ancient art.

DRILL STICK MYSTERIES

The stick end rests in the palm. The hands go back and forth in a figure-of-8 pattern. This turns the stick clockwise + anti-clockwise, but the hands don't 'walk' down it.

1. **The entry trick for the hand drill is making a figure-eight pattern—called "floating hands"—with your hands at the end of the drill so they don't ride down it. Instead of just rubbing your hands together back and forth with the stick in between, keep the**

end of the stick in your palm and make a rocking back-and-forth movement with each hand as well as rotating the stick between them. The hands won't creep down the drill but will stay in one place. Keeping the hands in one place on the drill enables you to drill continuously and raise the temperature to start the wood smoking. You may have to revert to walking down the drill with your hands to get enough pressure right at the end, but the floating hands technique is your staple. Practicing it often so that your hands toughen up is essential for avoiding nasty blisters.

Hand drilling is tricky...
It is MUCH easier in warm, dry weather!
sometimes there **is** smoke without fire...
baseboard

Baseboard hole is enlarged by drilling. Then a notch is cut to allow more air, and as a place for the hot dust.
The glowing coal in the dust

2. The rub-pat barrier is matching rotation with downward force. Too much rotation—using the figure-eight method—means not enough downforce to create friction. Too much downward force means the hands move fast down the drill (a long drill helps here) and then you have to wait while you stop and get back to the top to start drilling again.

3. The best baseboard material is made from clematis wood, the best drill from elder. Make sure both are collected from

dead wood that isn't rotten. If you have to cut it from live wood, dry it in the airing cupboard for a month or two. Damp is your biggest enemy when using a hand drill so practice in a dry place, off the damp floor—maybe on a bench in a garage or in your kitchen, if you can stand the smoke!

4. There are few things more satisfying than making fire with your own skill and a few pieces of wood. And the hand drill is the ultimate way to make fire when it comes to skill. Not many bushcraft instructors have mastered the hand drill. Expert Rich Lisney took three months practicing every time he got a spare moment in his kitchen. But what a great skill to have! Everyone is interested to see how it is done, an incentive perhaps to improve and get better.

5. Competitive hand-drilling is one way to break through the barrier. Start with a partner and race to see who can make the fire first.

6. Experiment with the size of the notch and different kinds of wood. Once you get good you may find almost any kind of wood can start a fire. Such knowledge is a great boon to anyone interested in bushcraft and outdoor living. Through the hand drill you can enter into a deeper knowledge of the landscape and the trees that populate it.

32

Make Your Handwriting Beautiful

In the age of computers people value a handwritten card or note highly. Many love to keep a diary or notebook full of ideas and observations. But if you can't read it, or if it's embarrassing to look at, then better handwriting is the answer. But not just better—beautiful.

1. **The entry tricks—there are two that will improve your writing. Instantly. First, hold your pen higher. Poor handwriters scribble with their mucky paws only millimeters from the nib. Hold it higher. Really high. Imagine it is a paint brush and you are Gauguin poised before the easel . . . holding a pen higher means you stop simply using the wrist and fingers and start using the whole arm. The more of the arm you can use, the better the handwriting. It will feel freer and look much better. The second trick is even more mysterious—simply elongate the letters with long tops and bottoms—make your "y"s and "p"s and "g"s with really long tails. Make your "t"s and "l"s and "h"s reach for the sky. You will straight away discover that not only does your writing look far better and more stylish but also that it no longer slopes down or up across the page. The reason is that every time you make a long letter you are sending a strong signal to the brain about where your pen is in relation to the page. It's as if you are recalibrating each time. When you scribble**

along with each letter at the same height, you have an initial starting reference, but then it's as if you are walking ahead without any guidelines.

2. The rub-pat barrier is speed versus beauty. But actually writing very slowly, like drawing slowly, can result in some ugly shapes. So you need to get up the speed yet keep the accuracy. This is best maintained through flourishes, through doing letters you really enjoy and actively look forward to writing. First, start with the elongated finials on "y"s and "t"s—and only do these. Do your little "a" with a top curl—like a printed one—it looks great and is very satisfying. But even better is doing a "g" like a printed one—a circle connected to a larger lower circle. It's almost impossible to make a "g" like this look bad and it gives your handwriting an extra element of interest and art.

3. Tools. Cheap paper and ballpoint pens lead one down the path of bad handwriting. Buy a fountain pen, a good one. The Japanese brand Sailor make some excellent writing pens—get the fine nib, it's more versatile. Get a nice notebook, maybe handmade. With the right materials you'll make more of an effort. If it's essential to keep the lines straight, rule very light pencil lines first.

4. Keep a diary with a view to showing it to others. Write short entries but make them beautiful. Include sketches and maps, if you like—somehow, writing always improves if it accompanies illustrations, however basic. Dan Price's *How to*

Make a Journal of Your Life (Ten Speed Press, 1999) is excellent reading on this subject.

5. Buy weird, odd, old, and interesting postcards whenever you can. Make a point of using them to stay in touch rather than e-mail. It's also a great way to make sure someone actually gets the message—even CEOs and celebrities get to see all their postcards since they might actually be from a close friend. But use each postcard as a chance to do nice handwriting.

6. When you have mastered the long finials and the "a"s and "g"s take a look at a book of copperplate and other handwriting styles. Look at some of the styles from centuries past. Copy them. With a high-held pen and a shoulder-led flourish they will be easy to master.

33

Micromaster Bargaining

The most pure and unadulterated form that bargaining can take is in an oriental bazaar or souk. Nothing has a marked price or a fixed price and everything, everything, is negotiable. Lots of great tricks can be learned here that can be applied elsewhere—from buying big things like cars and houses to negotiating a pay rise at work.

1. **The entry trick is simple—never hold what you want to buy. All stallholders know that psychologically holding a thing nurtures a grain of ownership in the mind of the holder, a nugget they can exploit and work with. By simply never holding the thing you want you create a powerful starting position—you can poke at it with a pen if you like, or, if desperate, make it one of several that you examine—thus watering down the act of holding.**

2. **Bargaining is all about information and perception barriers. If you know the real price of a thing then you are 80 percent ahead immediately. Information is everything, and you should use every method to obtain as much of it as you can. Going into a market blind is the easiest way to be robbed blind . . . except you may accidentally stumble on a well-kept secret. A friend of mine once offered a price a hundred times lower than that being asked for an ornamental knife in**

an Iranian market. He was just messing about. But in actuality the knives were obscenely marked up for tourists. The seller suddenly thought my friend knew the real price—so he sold it at this unbelievable discount. Of course, it is a finely played game—if you cannot conceal your desire for an object, it will upset your control of the situation, giving the seller the advantage. One way around this is to say in a smarmy voice, "I love this, but I'm going to be very cheeky and offer you . . ."

3. When it comes to moving your offer, you can be very sticky and move far less than the seller does. But, really, once an initial price has been mentioned you are unlikely to leave this ballpark. Your first offer is what really sets the whole thing up. If many shops are selling the same item—carved chess sets or inlaid boxes, all probably from the same makers—then go around minutely raising your offer with each until you get a bite. Again it's all about information—if you go into any bargaining situation thinking about this rather than "beating" the seller you'll leave behind all the emotional baggage that actually hinders getting a good deal. Because we all know that the best deals are made by those who can take it or leave it.

4. An antiques dealer once taught me there are two kinds of bargaining—the one-off strike and the back-and-forth to a happy medium. When you know the real price, when the seller knows you know the real price, go straight in with the real price. This can work better than back and forth because

you are demonstrating you have information, which will collapse some of the seller's confidence. Back-and-forthing paradoxically shows a lack of information—though beginners think it shows how "tough" they are.

5. If you're a tourist and look like a tourist, but you know the real price, don't expect to get it. It's not just information—perception plays a role too. When the seller thinks you can pay X he will dig his heels in. Sometimes he'd rather not sell than make an exception and treat a tourist like an insider. If you hand over a card to a stallholder that reveals you are also a dealer, you'll always get a discount. By selling cheaper to an insider, the stallholder is no longer losing face. But the main point is to practice a lot by buying lots of small, cheap items. Use "making a collection" as an excuse for getting good at bargaining.

6. Time and money are interchangeable. If there are many items the same in a market, then you have all the time in the world. Take your time and drive the price down. But if there is only one, and you like it, then time is not on your side. And if you don't have information, then you are vulnerable. This is when you can try the wild card. This is where you do the opposite of all the above. You say how much you love it. You caress the object. You say you must have it. You act over the top. But when you search through every pocket you only have a pittance. Sometimes this works. Stallholders are human too and prefer to sell to people they like.

34

Hone a Kitchen Knife So That It Is Razor Sharp

Sharp tools are a joy to use. Unfortunately, the kind of knife sharpeners that involve dragging the blade back and forth between wheels of ceramic or steel will only get a blade so-so sharp. It won't slice hairs off the back of your wrist, it won't be RAZOR sharp. And razor sharp is what you need if you want to chop and slice like a real pro.

1. The reason why almost all knives you buy will never achieve razor sharpness, including many fancy so-called chef's knives, is that they don't have a razor-style edge. They have a two-part edge. There is a low-angle slant that looks like the blade, but actually the edge is a much steeper angled "V" about a millimeter up from the cutting part of the blade. The trick is—first get rid of that secondary edge to make the "V" continuous from top to bottom of the blade. This takes work if you do it by hand using a file or a very rough Japanese water stone because you are removing quite a bit of metal.

2. A super-rough Japanese water stone is the easiest way to remove a lot of metal if you don't have access to a slow grinder. A very fast grinder may alter the temper of your blade. The best stones have water running over them and allow the easy removal of metal. But a rough stone will

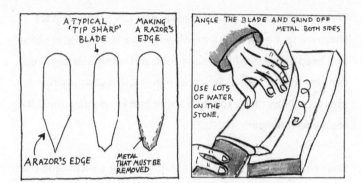

A TYPICAL 'TIP SHARP' BLADE

MAKING A RAZOR'S EDGE

A RAZOR'S EDGE

METAL THAT MUST BE REMOVED

ANGLE THE BLADE AND GRIND OFF METAL BOTH SIDES

USE LOTS OF WATER ON THE STONE.

work: just take your time. You can use circles or drag the blade across the stone. Do exactly the same number on each side to keep the angle the same on both sides. If you drag ten times on one side, drag ten on the other. You know it is working because at first the knife will seem blunter, not sharper. You just have to keep going. When it at last seems sharper you can stop removing metal. You should at this stage see there is now a straight "V" from the edge up both sides and not an angled "V" as before.

3. The hard part is knowing how hard to push down as you drag the knife across the water stone—the rub-pat barrier. Too much pressure and you'll scour chunks out of the stone and even the knife edge. Too little and it won't work. Imagine spreading butter on toast, butter that is not frozen but not over-soft. Assign numbers in your head to the differing levels of pressure you use. You learn a lot about how much pressure is correct when taking the metal off using the very rough stone. This knowledge will help in the next two stages.

4. Once you have that straight edge, you can properly start sharpening. Begin with a medium-grit Japanese water stone and keep going until the blade feels definitely sharper. You can test it by dragging it across paper without applying pressure. Now move to a fine stone and keep going until it feels even sharper.

5. You're now ready to strop the blade—using a technique that old-time barbers use. Get a thick leather belt and thoroughly wet it. Loop it around your foot and hold it tight. You now (carefully) slap the blade back and forth, first one side then the other, on the wet leather. This smooths out all the tiny points raised by the sharpening on the stone. Instead of having an edge that resembles a saw when viewed through a microscope, it will look more like a . . . razor.

6. Once you've sharpened one knife to razor-like perfection, try it on chisels and plane blades. The whole experience of woodwork, like cookery, is completely different with really sharp tools.

35

Lead a Small Group in the Wilderness

If you can micromaster leading a small group in the wilderness, you can lead any kind of group anywhere. Not for nothing do managers send their trainees on outward-bound courses. The wilderness is the unknown by definition, and leaders are paid to guide people in places where they don't know where to go or when and where to stop. This is the first and main definition of a leader. Forget the nonsense about charisma and passion and commitment—the leader is simply the person who knows the way and the correct manner of traveling. This could be knowing the exact route or it could include hiring a local guide—in either case they make the final decisions about which way to go and when to start and stop.

Why wilderness leading is so useful a training is that someone in the group always knows better. One member is secretly after your job. Not that they will actually WANT it once they have it; it is just an inalienable fact in group dynamics that the leader is there to be replaced. Probably it's a healthy guard against despotism—however, if you aren't aware of this then you could lose everything. Because there is no rank or outside enforced status and no one is being paid to take orders, this form of leadership is very pure. The desire to take over—which will manifest itself in any work environment too, but more subtly—is out in the open.

1. The entry trick is simple—you control the map. The map reader knows the way. If you have a GPS, control that too. And have a watch with an alarm so you can wake up early. Ignore all other sources of route information. Explain that people suggesting different routes is not helpful. This connects to the next fact—lead from the front. Be the point man or woman. Because in every trip the path will diverge and someone will have to make a decision—that's your job.

2. Leaders know more than anyone else. Leaders are the teachers of the group. If someone knows more than you, appoint them the expert in that area. But only you can decide where you are going and when you stop. It doesn't matter if you pass a lovely bit of ground that looks ideal for a rest stop—if you haven't made the distance you need to, then you keep going, despite the protests. Popularity helps, but wilderness leadership is about getting the group from A to B in one piece. That's all.

3. The rub-pat barrier is mixing with the troops and maintaining isolation. The more you know in detail about the route, the stronger you are about everything you are likely to meet, and so the more you can afford to get pally. It always helps to have a number two, an adjutant-type figure. Together you form an unstoppable bulwark against the massed ranks of naysayers. You can be friendly to your adjutant and a bit distant with the others. Without distance it's very hard to get people to do things they don't want to do. If you get drunk and fall over the night before, don't be

surprised if they question your route finding the next day. This is important because a lot of the time you might not have much confidence in yourself. To boost that confidence you need the confidence of others. On the other hand, if you make a mistake, it doesn't mean you have to give up the map.

4. Assign jobs, make everyone equal, rotate the jobs, and do your exact share. Eat after everyone else has eaten and be the first person up every morning. It doesn't matter how late you go to bed as long as you are the first up. You'll have to be the hurrier and goader if you want to leave on time—and if you haven't set a time, you won't be.

5. As an experiment, go on a hike with friends of differing abilities and debate every part of the route, when and where to stop: see what happens. It may well be more fun than leading but you won't make the miles you planned. If all the members of the small group are equally skilled and the objective is very clear—as in climbing a mountain—you'll find they need less leading.

36

Learn to Read Japanese in Three Hours

Japanese has three alphabets and is a super-hard language by re-
pute, and yet there is a way to micromaster it. The kanji, or Chinese characters used in Japanese, number in the thousands, though
a basic high-school graduate's knowledge is 1,945. The hiragana is
a syllabic alphabet which has only forty-six symbols. It is used for
writing words of Japanese origin other than those for which there
is a complete Chinese character. Katakana is another syllabic alphabet, also with forty-six symbols, which is used for writing
words of foreign origin—like your name or items on a food menu
such as hamburger or pizza or ramen noodle. Katakana is the best
to learn first because you can immediately start decoding Japanese signs that often have many foreign words in them.

1. **The entry trick is to go and buy James Heisig's masterful book
    on learning the katakana.* He has written a couple of books
    on learning kanji too. When he was a student, he devised a
    very smart mnemonic system that enables you to memorize
    Japanese symbols and then build on them systematically.**

2. **Heisig's book is short and it will take you less than three
    hours to learn and memorize the katakana. Though there are**

---

* James Heisig, *Remembering the Kana: Hiragana and Katakana* (Japan Publications Trading Co., 2001).

forty-six symbols, there are only a few basic shapes. You can learn these and then build on them. You'll immediately be able to read foreign words in manga comics and on menus and shop signs. You'll be able to write your name and be able to show that skill off to any Japanese you meet. I found that using a brush made it more fun to learn Japanese characters. Pentel makes pens that have an ink cartridge and a brush head so that it is like a brush that you don't have to dip into ink. Getting in the mood and feeling more Japanese all helps the learning.

3. Heisig has his own mnemonic system but devise your own to run in parallel. For example, the sign for RA really looks like a half bowl with something on top—in other words a RAmen soup with a piece of pork on top. The sign for the syllable RO is a square—in other words a ROund that has been squared off. The sign for SU looks like a SoUp bowl with a spoon leaning against its side.

4. The crazier and wilder the mnemonic system the better. The sign for NA looks like two thin lines of a mustache— something that is Not Acceptable in Japan (as only some men can grow decent ones).

5. Look at the syllable sheet and have fun making up your own ways to remember things. If you get interested, move on to hiragana—this is used for very common Japanese words and word endings and also in some manga where kanji is deemed "too difficult."

37

Become a Street Photographer

Street photography goes in fashionable phases—but the rise of small, discreet, and high-resolution digital cameras has brought it within the purview of anyone, rather than the more exclusive Leica-wielding minority it previously appealed to.

1. The entry trick is simply GET CLOSER. If you focus on something (if you have time), take a brave two or three steps forward before you fire the shutter. Get REALLY close to people and use them as the foreground to something interesting going on beyond. Set the camera at a high aperture and film speed and that will leave more in focus.

2. The rub-pat barrier is between speed and wobble/lack of focus. While you can intentionally include blur in your pictures, there are some to which camera shake just doesn't add anything. It helps to watch top street photographer Daidō Moriyama at work (lots of videos on YouTube). Though he shoots very fast and often from the hip without sighting up through the viewfinder, he stops in his path just for a fraction to get the shot steady. Though he has a "walking style" of shooting as opposed to the more static Cartier-Bresson method of finding a good background and waiting for something interesting to happen in front of it (a

bike passing, a bunch of kids playing, etc.), he still knows that pressing the shutter on the move in front of a possibly moving subject is very likely to produce blur (even at 1/500 shutter speed, walking fast toward another walker can produce blur). You need courage of a sort to poke a camera in someone's face and hold it still. But it doesn't need to be offensive. Cartier-Bresson covered his in black tape so that the camera was less visible, and he perfected a way of sneakily taking shots so that people hardly noticed. Moriyama is similarly careful. "I don't want to hurt people's feelings," he explains.

3. In photography the nerds are right—at first it is ALL about the kit. This doesn't mean it has to be expensive, it just has to be right for you and make you want to take photos. For some that can be an iPhone or other device—you are encouraged by its ubiquity to take photos where you otherwise would not. A small camera that is quick to focus and is very quiet is perfect. If you can fit it in your pocket you'll carry it a whole lot more than if it has to be slung over your shoulder. Get one with good low-light capability—up to 25,000 ISO if you can. An SLR with a big hulking zoom— forget it—you'll get lazy and keep your distance. A wide-angle lens—less than 30 mm if possible—will force you to conquer that rub-pat barrier of getting closer, faster.

4. The payoff can come from Flickr, Facebook, Instagram, or whatever social media platform is currently the place to

show off street pictures. Load up as many as you can. Let others decide how good they are. You'll be surprised.

5. Digital photography is even more repeatable and addictive than film photography. You can take a hundred pictures a day very easily, day after day. And if you do, you'll get better very quickly. Just carry the camera everywhere—even to the supermarket or the library, and especially at night.

6. Experimental possibilities are endless. Color, black-and-white, or using filters. And in processing you can saturate colors or—my favorite—whack up the contrast. You may be led, as I was, back from digital and into film photography—a great world of experiment and creativity awaits!

38

Brew Delicious Craft Beer

Gone are the days when homebrew was synonymous with cheap and buttery-flavored beer. Now homebrewers can equal and even exceed the productions of well-regarded mainstream breweries. In 2014 Graham Nelson, who had been brewing for only a year, produced a homemade 5.3 percent India pale ale which so impressed the judges of a homebrew competition that it was copied by Thornbridge Brewery and put on sale at most branches of Waitrose under the moniker Vienna IPA.

Beer can be drunk very soon (sometimes only a few days) after it is made. This means you can repeat quickly and learn as you go. There is plenty of room for micromastery experimentation with each batch you make. We recommend, though, that you stick to a single beer type—IPA—and just keep making that until it is perfect.

There is a vast amount on the internet about craft brewing—what we supply here is enough to get you started.

1. **The entry trick—which was used by Graham Nelson—is to use an all-grain complete brewing kit. This replicates exactly what a major brewery does to make beer, only in miniature. You can buy such kits—which will last for many years—for between $200 and $400. Once you have one, it is perfectly possible to produce a beer that will be the envy of any brewery.**

2. Once you have the all-grain kit, use only the best ingredients you can find, again mimicking the methods used by good established breweries. Don't feel you always have to use local hops and malt—use what is best for the recipe you have. Use wet yeast rather than the dry yeast that homebrewers in the past always made do with. There are several suppliers who can provide the homebrewer with top-quality ingredients—www.brewersselect.co.uk, for example. In order to make a good IPA, search online for a detailed recipe that others have found works well. A good place to start is beersmith.com but there is no shortage of information about craft brewing online.

3. Things which will help get you there faster: as we suggest, try an IPA as your first beer. Its flavor includes small amounts of diacetyl, an offshoot of the fermentation process which in excess produces an almost popcorn-like butterscotch flavor that also nastily coats the tongue during drinking. Lagers require careful handling to remove the diacetyl but this refinement isn't so crucial with an IPA, thus simplifying the process. Clean everything meticulously— brewing is 90 percent cleaning, some say—and if you use the right cleaning products, such as Star San no-rinse cleaner, you'll get rid of the trace bacteria that can wreak havoc with the flavor.

4. Homebrewers still have one advantage over the big boys— whenever you serve your beer, you can add alcohol and flavorings and even blend with other beers to get the taste

you want. It's demoralizing to have people mock your beer, so if you need to mix it secretly with something else beforehand, do it! This kind of experimentation is how you learn the basic way flavors come about in beer. After changing the flavor at the point of drinking, you can later start to adapt the process so you can build in the desired flavor at the beginning.

you easily to jamming through it. With people who, you back so if you need to mix it up or vary with something they experiment, new start. These students know you with the basic skills, they compound, in steel. After changing the flavor of the point of drink up, you catalyst.

39

Make Your Own Shirt

Look on the Web and you'll see people saying that shirt-making is way beyond them. Forget this and jump straight in. This is one of those micromasteries where you attack a self-limiting idea. Like John-Paul Flintoff, you can make your first shirt in about ten hours—maybe less. So set aside ten hours in a single day. A shirt in a day: wow!

1. **The entry trick is to take a favorite shirt and copy each panel onto paper. The collar, the shoulders, the arms, the cuffs. Don't buy a pattern, as they can be confusing to a raw beginner—instead, make your own from paper that is quite thick. Next, unpick an old shirt into its component bits. You'll get a good idea from this about how much extra cloth to leave as you stitch each part together. Now find the cloth you want to use—two square meters will allow you plenty and a little extra in case of mistakes. Draw around each paper panel onto the cloth lightly with chalk (or pin the pattern to the cloth and cut around it, leaving an edge for stitching). Then carefully cut it out with SHARP scissors. Lay all the pieces out. See, it's just like an IKEA kit—dead easy.**

2. **If you are really simplicity-minded, you could hand-sew it. This is a good skill that is still used in top fashion houses. But that will take considerably longer than ten hours. Instead,**

get a sewing machine that is simple and reliable. This could even be a manual sewing machine if electric motors and sharp needles freak you out. Certainly, there is a greater sense of control with a hand-turned or treadle sewing machine. But modern electric machines are very easy to use. The main thing is, the machine should inspire you and make you want to get stitching. There are lots of simple, reliable sewing machines for sale on eBay. And the internet will have the manual online. Download it and find out how to do the simplest stitch for shirt making: the lockstitch.

Now practice sewing straight lines of lockstitch. Feed the cloth steadily through and, like magic, a line of stitching appears. The important thing is to let the machine do the work. You don't need to push or pull the cloth, simply keep it in line. Try stitching a tube of cloth such as that used for an arm piece. Scrunch up the cloth so that you can sew its entire length. The rub-pat barrier in machine-sewing is balancing the speed you sew at (which affects the speed of the cloth moving) with the accuracy of the stitching. But don't worry—if you go off course, you can use the seam ripper to clear that line of stitching and start again.

3. Get cloth that really excites you to make the shirt—the crazier the better, if that is what gets you going. Non-stretchy cotton is easiest, though. Very thin cloth will be harder to handle as it may stretch out of shape as you sew. Once you have practiced machine-stitching long enough that you can do fairly straight lines, it is time to begin assembling the shirt. Iron each piece as you assemble it.

Have the iron hot and ready to use as you go. You'll need it to get rid of wrinkles and also to make hems and folded bits. Start with making the two front panels—both will need foldovers at the point they will meet—you will see how from the shirt you disassembled. You can tack pieces together very quickly by hand-sewing, or you can use pins. Tacking takes longer but it is a little easier than to machine sew. So, pin or tack the edges that need sewing to hold the cloth in place. Sew the front and the back pieces to the shoulder yoke. Next do the buttonholes (hand-sew these or use the buttonhole-stitching attachment on the machine). Next do the armholes, sides stitched to the back, sleeves, cuffs, and collar.

4. The hard part as you go along is not giving up because your shirt doesn't look like a real one. Remember, it hasn't been pressed yet—that can make a huge difference to what it looks like.

5. As soon as it is ready, press it and wear it. You might even stitch your own designer label above the pocket that reads "I made it all myself." After a shirt, micromaster John-Paul Flintoff made a pair of jeans—I've seen them and you couldn't tell they weren't made by a top designer.

Micromaster
Your Life

Permission to Be Interested

Start small, start humble. As children we all started by learning how to do a few small things well—using cutlery, tying our shoelaces, riding a bicycle. Can this essentially low-key approach be leveraged into a way to improve almost everything about your life? I think it can.

This book makes the alluring promise of revealing a hidden path to happiness. It's hidden because we hide it from ourselves. We hide that which is too difficult, complex, expensive, time-consuming. The hidden is all we deny ourselves permission to be interested in.

Everything starts with interest. If we aren't interested we don't notice and we don't learn. Happy people have interests and are interesting, and showing severe lack of interest is a sign of depression.

Yet no one gives us *permission* to be interested.

That's right. The culture we live in tantalizes through images, and yet tacitly withdraws any genuine involvement. The "real world" is presented as professional—there to be admired, but not touched. So the hidden path to success is relearning how to give yourself permission to be interested and engaged . . . in anything.

This world is a complex place, good at shutting people out, excluding them, making people exclude themselves. Though it might be necessary, say, to exclude a person with dirty hands from an operating room, much of life is not like this. In most of our lives, we could all be a lot more interested and a lot more involved.

We don't do it, usually, because the entry costs in terms of energy, commitment, money, kit, knowledge, and so on are seen as too high. And we get into the habit. We imagine things. A man who built a car for $350 found that no one asked him how many hours it took or how difficult it was to do. They all commented on how hard it was going to be to get it licensed for the road. Actually, that was the easy part (DMV officials are bored and love giving something new a chance to be used). But people are used to thinking that "red tape" is stopping them.

And it's a lot easier to watch the latest box set instead of actually doing something.

Micromastery, as a way of looking at the world, gives you unlimited permission to be interested, unlimited permission to get involved. Welcome to the limitless world.

The tiger and the cage

Imagine a tiger locked in a cage—a roaring tiger, eager to escape. That roaring tiger is all the bundled energy and enthusiasm you have, just waiting to be unleashed upon the world. Doesn't it feel like that sometimes? That if only you could find the right key to the cage all your indecision, indolence, and lack of gumption would disappear, and that roaring tiger would be unstoppable . . .

The cage has two doors. Both locked. One door is big and inviting with a single large keyhole. The other small and a tight squeeze with three locks. The floor of the cage is littered with keys and the poor tiger, with his clumsy old paws, has a hard enough time just lifting a key and fitting it in the lock. Some are big keys and some are little keys. The big keys seem the obvious ones, even though they are much heavier, harder to find, and harder to handle. After a huge amount of effort the tiger finds a big key and unlocks the big door.

The big door leads to a place full of food. It seems wonderfully free at first. He gorges on all the food and grows awfully big and fat and clumsy. But then he slowly discovers he has simply entered a larger cage. Once he starts looking, he finds there is an exit—no key required, but it is very small and low and he can't fit through it. Moreover, now he finds that all the fine food is both sickening and addictive. He can't lose weight and his former boundless energy begins to wane, he grows tired and old and even scared of the world outside. Too late he realizes that the job, career, specialization is merely a means to an end—to being able to interact with the world with energy and enthusiasm. But he thought it was an end in itself, and by his thinking that, it became another cage.

The smaller, less distinguished door requires three different keys. But there are many on the ground. Any three will do. Quickly the tiger learns all you have to do is find and insert one, and then another, and another . . . it's easy. Soon the little door is unlocked. Into a place with just enough meager food to keep him looking and learning. He, too, finds that he is in another cage but also quickly finds the small exit. Still slim and fit he bounds through it. And through this exit lies the whole abundant world. Truly free, the tiger's energy and enthusiasm never wanes. He is OPEN, ON, he has permission to be interested in everything. He can even do the job, career, and specialization because he knows that it's not the answer to everything. He has permission to be interested in the abundant world.

The object in life is not mastery over one subject—attractive though that is. There are many masters of one thing—from sport to art to business—who live wasted and unhappy lives. The object is to use mastery to get out of the cage and live the fullest life you can. That means becoming more polymathic, more open, more alive. You get out of the cage by using micromasteries to give yourself permission to be interested and involved in anything you want, and to be able to withhold and extend interest, and switch interest with fluency and ease.

You've always felt like this.

Inside you there is a caged tiger of energy and enthusiasm just waiting to burst out. Release that tiger!

Your Many Selves

Your passport, ID cards, driver's license, and bank accounts all have the same name on them. You are doomed to be that one person. Our whole culture underpins this notion, yet it is blatantly untrue—you are not one, you are many.

The insights of multiple-personality psychology provide a useful metaphor for us all. We house many different selves; just a moment's reflection will reveal that. One of our selves might like smoking, while the rest hate it. You might have a self who loves sports, yet there is another who loves to curl up with a book and abhors the idea of moving even to get a drink of water. One self might be interested in poetry and art, another might revel in business and making money. And all these selves jostle and rapidly succeed one another throughout the day.

If you are uncomfortable with the idea of multiple selves at this point, think of them as "strands of self." But they are strands with considerable autonomy—just as a single strand of a rope is similar to, but more limited than, the rope itself.

Who hasn't felt exasperation at hearing they're either introverted or extroverted? Most of us can be both, depending on the situation and the self in charge.

Sometimes you can start in one self and be jerked into another, and the results can be dramatic—suddenly you're in the groove and really humming. Some of your selves may be good at driving and some not—it can be as simple as that when it comes to having a collision on the road. The first step is simply to *accept the idea* you are many, not one. Then simply observe these different selves in action, how often they crop up and what they are good and not so good at.

Identify your many selves through micromastery

Micromastery works as the visible, experiential evidence of the multiple strands of self. Each micromastery we feel drawn to learn represents a self. I felt a need to practice martial arts, just as I did with drawing, long-distance walking, writing, and cooking. They are all strands of my rope.

But the self isn't just a series of mundane skills. We have to empathize with, be interested in, and care for others. We have to build and sometimes destroy. A carpenter and a blacksmith must have a violent self in order to wield the tools they use at work. A gardener must have a self that is patient and caring.

All these selves can be represented by micromasteries too, or be an integral part of one.

What gives you pleasure? Observe your little routines. Some may have developed already into full-blown interests, while others might be nascent, waiting to be activated.

Observe yourself as you undertake different activities. Look for the things you do and don't enjoy that seem to crop up while doing those things. Different selves have different likes. One might enjoy mixing with all kinds of people, picking up new ideas for businesses. Another, who may surface after a few hours of fiction writing, is "recluse," who doesn't even want to leave the apartment. If "recluse" is forced outside and made to do heavy exercise—like running up a hillside—he may flip into "mountain man," a self who likes nothing better than grueling physical exertion.

All change begins with observation, which must be done without judgment. It cannot be repeated too many times that controlling these selves starts with this, rather than a desire to change.

Once you've observed them, assign each self a micromastery, if it hasn't got one already. If you have a controlling, tidying, finishing self, assign it a task like washing up, cleaning shoes, ironing—something satisfying and limited. Maybe turn shoe shining into a micromastery. Then, should you need to become more controlling and finishing, just clean some shoes to get into that frame of mind.

The recent boom in adult coloring books is fascinating. Coloring offers a way to activate that detail-loving, manually skilled side of the brain we are denied using in so many keyboard-based jobs. The coloring micromastery is being used to access a different self, one that is more relaxed and has more fun.

Kung Fu Panda—the first and best movie in the franchise—has the wonderful sequence where Shifu (voiced by Dustin Hoffman) is angrily intoning "inner peace, inner PEACE, INNER PEACE!" The message is clear—we can't command our emotional state through mere words or wishful thinking. The multiple-self model makes it obvious why—we need to enter a different self, not calm down. When we flip into a new self we calm down immediately.

Ever gone out and chopped wood when you're angry? Flipping to a physical self works wonders. Who hasn't seen the immediate effect good news can have? I once was in bed with the flu and received news that I had got a new job. I leaped out of bed and was "cured" immediately. Another self had taken over. I am not suggesting all illness can disappear so easily, but being in the wrong self for certain situations exacerbates stresses that can lead to illness. Once you embrace rather than fight against the multiple-self model, you actively look for ways to switch, and you can use a micromastery to do so.

When you can flip to the best self for the job you will find tasks so much easier. For example, because I was overawed by the martial arts environment in Japan I was in "student" mode a lot of the time. But actually, in order to do something physical it was far better to be in a "tough physical guy" frame of mind. Now, when I have to do a physical learning task, I practice skill and balancing warm-up exercises, sometimes to exhaustion—anything that leads away from the more inner-directed self used in writing. Conversely, I use the reflective task of writing about the best moment of the previous day as a way of entering my writing self.

Micromaster the harmonica

Nick Reynolds is the son of great train robber Bruce Reynolds, who, after committing the biggest robbery of the time in 1963, eventually gave himself up and went to prison for twelve years. Nick grew up without a father present, and made an early vow never to follow the same path and end up behind bars—he saw what a waste that was of any person's potential. He saw the Royal

Navy as both an honorable profession and a way to lead an exciting but worthwhile existence. Soon after signing up he found himself fighting in the Falklands, where he served on battleships under constant attack from the Argentine Air Force.

Though he might have imagined he had a single self—the professional sailor—it became apparent that in periods of downtime other selves come to the fore, and they demanded release. Nick found himself being more rebellious, bucking against the routines of the navy. The rebel self can take pleasure in spoiling all your other selves' best efforts. But rebel selves can be turned toward either destructive or creative micromasteries. If we are lucky, art is where we go when we rebel against the tedious normality of everyday life—and artistic micromasteries have rehabilitated many people.

Nick was musical but didn't have the inclination or time to learn a complicated instrument, so he picked one of the easiest—the harmonica. Also, though he hadn't been to art school, he could still draw—as everyone can. So he kept himself busy in the navy by playing the harmonica and drawing—both skills which, as they developed, people remarked upon.

He realized gradually that the navy was a kind of trap for a creative soul. He needed more freedom to explore the gifts he'd developed. As an artist he started drawing and then casting in bronze the heads of famous criminals that his father had known. He also cast the head of any famous criminal who died, thus reviving the ancient art of making death masks. Nick wanted to use this as a way of drawing attention to the wrong choices criminals made, though many people saw it as the opposite, as aggrandizing the criminal fraternity.

Through his art Nick managed to attend many parties given by the bohemian creative types living in London. At one such party he deployed his other micromastery—playing the harmonica—and people liked it. When the pop group Alabama 3 needed a harmonica player they thought of Nick, bringing him into the band and giving him a second string to add to his career as an artist. Each activity helped the other—through his work in the music business he was able to get more commissions for his sculptures. A moment of recognition was when an Alabama 3 music track was chosen as the theme for the hit TV series *The Sopranos*.

Honor thy selves

No one is born a lawyer, doctor, plumber, or baker. We braid our multiple selves into one fairly convincing rope and then hope the world won't notice the joins.

We can do this by trying to kill various strands, various selves we have. We can do it by ignoring their many pleas for recognition. We can do it by compartmentalizing our lives. Or we can do it by trying to integrate as best we can the warring selves into one coherent whole.

Traditional wisdom the world over suggests that trying to integrate our various personalities into one that is aligned with a general purpose, "a path," is best. There is little to disagree with here. The only problem is: How do you identify your many different selves in the first place? And how do you keep tabs on them?

I think that we need to honor and recognize each self as part of us. You can't just sweep one bit of you under the mat and hope it'll stay hidden. An author may go through phases where the writer self takes control. This self revels in spending long hours bashing away at the keyboard. It resents having to get exercise and talk to others, and particularly hates e-mail. After a while all the other selves begin to resent writer self's draconian rule. One day writer self will flip—there is usually some catalyst, a sunny day, a forced trip or journey, even a new hairstyle can do it—then bang, another personality takes over. It could be exercise and adventure self, or accountant self (who is generally despised until bills need paying), or mariner self, who wants only to set sail across the high seas . . .

Crushing your various selves works temporarily, then they come back and start fighting for position again. But if they have a micromastery associated with them, you can start to control them. Think of them as an unruly family fighting for attention—until they have been recognized and honored they are not so easy to deal with.

Your various selves may surprise you. They may appear trivial to you, even superficial. You might have a self that revels in fashion and coiffure, though you really believe these things are beneath you. You may have a self that loves making things, simple things like jigsaws or model aircraft. After all, both David Beckham and Norman Mailer honor a Lego-building self . . .

Punk Micromastery

The punk bands of the late 1970s and early '80s were famous for one thing: they sang and played really, really badly. They didn't, however, wait for permission. They worked around their limitations, writing simple songs that didn't need great skill to play. Yet many of those songs by the Clash and others are still great songs: classics created by unskilled musicians.

The punk mentality extended into writing. Mark Perry, aided by school friends Steve Micalef and Danny Baker, started their own fanzine dedicated to music, called *Sniffin' Glue*. Sold outside gigs, it became a hit and a huge influence in the world of music journalism. Danny Baker went on to become a music journalist and TV presenter, Micalef obtained a trade union scholarship to Oxford University based on the quality of his writing, and Mark Perry started the band ATV.

They wanted to publish a magazine so they got writing and photocopying and did it, even though none of them had any training or experience. In fact Micalef, who after Oxford became a performance poet, claimed he hadn't read an entire book until he was fifteen.*

The punk mentality insists, "Why not try it?" Instead of waiting around for the ideal moment, find a simplified version, a micromastery. Instead of learning to play the guitar, learn one song. Play it a lot. Experiment with it.

It's not uncommon to meet someone with a PhD doing a job that doesn't require one—journalism, for example. We see all kinds of qualification inflation going on. Why? Because people are too scared to just go out and do stuff. You don't need to go to school for twenty years to write for a newspaper or magazine (actually it will probably make you a worse writer). Though I am a fan of limited, specific courses that help you learn something, lengthy academic courses can be simply a great training ground for . . . more lengthy academic courses.

The punk mentality came with a fierce rejection of the contemporary music scene. There was an urge to be different from the pampered and exclusive rock and soul music of the time. So while the Sex Pistols dreamed of being rock stars, and even covered old rock and roll standards, they were rough and homemade in every sense.

Escaping the ordinary means taking a different path from everyone else. It means using DIY techniques to achieve what you want—right now—rather than waiting for years.

Micromastery shares the same urgency. The world threatens us with its rules and exclusions—break through them and do your

* *Reach for the Sky* by Paul Brickhill was that book.

own thing. Pick a micromastery and go for it. Instead of spending a fortune on a Chinese language course you'll probably give up, you can micromaster right now a simple set of greetings. Master all of them so you can greet everyone from an emperor to a small child. You'll have something permanent that you can also use as a springboard to learn much more.

Give yourself permission to be interested and involved by invoking the spirit of punk.

Micromastery vs Global Pessimism

Pessimism is showing a lurking preference for the negative and showering it with one's valuable store of interest-energy. Pessimism is a cheat—it takes our attention but denies us the chance to be involved. "Not worth it," the pessimist concludes. Of course there is bad stuff out there. But send your interest and involvement toward the light, the positive, the things that you know work. The optimist might join Doctors Without Borders as a doctor helping in disaster zones; the pessimist scans the internet and "likes" disaster news.

Pessimism is to be found anywhere people say they can't improve, learn, move on, change, lead, follow—it thrives in the land of *can't*. There is informed pessimism—for example when you've seen the weather forecast—and there is unnoticed inner pessimism. It is the latter which is the problem.

People self-limit and self-sabotage. With very little evidence they assume they'll be no good. So what if they are no good? The people who attended the tone-deaf singing course with me went on to sing on prime-time TV and get paid for it—though they were "no good," they were now professionals.

Inner pessimism thrives on self-limitation: "I haven't got time," "I'm only an amateur." It causes self-sabotage: "I'm not up to it so I won't go any more." This has to be the biggest cause of failure—not turning up because inner pessimism tells you that you aren't "good enough."

The global culture, and our national culture, has its own brand of pessimism. Consumer culture is inherently pessimistic. The underlying message is: shopping and eating and getting new stuff is the limit of our ambition. Remember that ad for Gillette razors: "the best a man can get"? Er, maybe not. Don't misunderstand me, there isn't some evil Dr. Ad-man pulling the wires, some corporation intent on destroying the minds of ordinary people; rather it is the result of logically trying to extract as much money as you can out of people using every legal means available. Wall-to-wall advertising naturally depicts characters who are attenuated in their passions, or who prefer to buy something rather than do something—and the drip-feed effect of this distorts the norm.

Our culture pimps and peddles this pessimism—it wants us to be passive consumers rather than superhuman producers. Look at those McDonald's ads—the world is portrayed as a crappy place where a Big Mac is the best you can aspire to. I'm lovin' it.

Success culture is pessimistic too

And yet our culture is obsessed with success. People who don't succeed are deemed losers. Some people self-identify as "beat" or "slacker," and they may even "succeed" in this role (though the original beatnik, Jack Kerouac, died an alcoholic at forty-nine with most of his books out of print; only later was he reimagined as a "success").

The trivial version of success culture, its basic model, is winning the lottery. The aim is always the same—you never have to work again. I once watched a self-important woman announce that she was now the "success" she always dreamed she'd be because she'd won $80 million in a state lottery. But she was just the same person she was before she won. Money, though very nice to have, is merely a kind of tool. It's like saying: now that I have a big digger, I am the success I have always dreamed of being. But what are you going to dig? And what are you going to do with that money? Buy a big house and a lot of cars? You're still a dork, with or without the trimmings.

People fantasize about buying big houses, land, farms—but they very often end up getting someone else to manage it for them. As a woodland officer at North York Moors National Park Authority, Mark Antcliff, told me, "You can't buy a lifestyle." People don't realize that the "dream job" actually requires a lot of hidden work, rather than just cash, to become the surface reality others see. It has been wisely asserted that life is less about "doing what one likes" and more about "liking what one does." You can find out what you like through micromastery, then do it.

Developing a micromastery costs very little. But measure this real success against the trivial success of winning the lottery. Naturally, I'd love the money too—the point is that it doesn't remove the need to find something to do. Its only virtue— widening your permission to be interested—is useless if you don't have the basic knowledge about how to micromaster your way into something you will like doing.

Unlike the weird vibe that emanates from "success culture," a combination of glorification and buried pessimism, most successful people are rather unexceptional and optimistic. They simply found what they liked doing and did a lot of it. Eventually, they also found a way to get paid doing it.

The innate pessimism of success culture says that "only successful people count," which goes hand in hand with the idea that "only other people succeed." But if we step aside from notions of how hard it is to succeed and instead look at building and developing our interests, talents, and skills, we'll see that the only real "success" is in improving yourself. Everything else is just stuff happening. A person who has learned things, cared for another person, honed a skill, taught someone, developed a talent, turned up and done something—that person can view their life as a real success.

Micromastery kicks the ass of pessimism every time. The whole premise is that everyone can try this—everyone can be a micromaster of many things. The number of micromasteries is almost limitless. I've detailed over thirty in this book, but that is only skimming the surface. Every area of sport, work, art, craft has its own potential micromasteries. And they are all out there just waiting for you to try. Fancy learning an Icelandic saga by heart (it'll go down a storm when you visit Reykjavik)? Well, get on and start now. Fancy learning how to wingsuit off a mountain? There are courses out there. Want to be a sushi king? A maker of sloe gin? It's all waiting—you have permission to be interested in everything and anything and you can pursue any micromastery you wish. This doesn't mean a lifetime commitment—just a short, sharp immersion. And you can stay for as long or as little as you desire.

Pessimism can bury you for years. Then one day you wake up and throw open the curtains and say, "Hey, this is an incredible world jammed full of amazing opportunities to become better at things, and become a better person." Micromastery rolls back the pessimism by giving you an edge, a real improvement. When you have micromastered something, no matter how down you get, it can't be taken away from you. It becomes part of your permanent, and positive, inheritance. You may be depressed and thinking, "My life is wasted," and then you'll remember, "Well at least I can do that, at least I did that." And from these small beginnings you can claw your way back up to a full realization of how abundant the opportunities are in life.

The BIG, BIGGER, BIGGEST Picture

So. You learn these micromasteries, become more polymathic, happier, more successful (in the widest sense, of course), but what is the really important reason for all this? It has to be the growth of the individual—you, me—measured in the degree of integration of your selves that you ultimately achieve.

It is no good overdeveloping one self at the expense of the others. It might serve some organization, army, cause, or family—you might be a good worker bee like those Japanese executives who die from overwork and dedication to their corporations—but that wasn't why you were put on this planet. We're not here for purely mundane earthbound reasons, and any motivation that misses the human need to connect to the greater mysteries of life is ultimately going to shortchange you.

To do this you need to be a better person—more integrated, less trivial, more perceptive, more empathetic, more resilient, more energetic. A single self obsessed by stock prices, beauty products, or toy trains can't run your real life. You know you are a whole gamut of selves and these need integrating to reach the next level of connection to the deeper realities of life.

Our multiple selves compete and demand recognition. But they also attack and belittle each other. When I am my business self and see a painting or photograph, I often unthinkingly dismiss it—yet if I was my artist self I would admire it. Business self wants to put down any other selves.

Take a moment and observe your different reactions to things. Take food: one self might like healthy food, but when the other self, who likes guiltier pleasures, is in the driving seat, this healthy food will be lampooned as inedible or boring. So not only do we lose energy and direction by switching selves, we also lose a lot more by attacking other selves. This is where attempts at integration begin.

To integrate all these disparate selves into one useful operating organism is like herding cats—or can be. What is required is a powerful and compelling overarching identity that can draw all these elements together. This identity has to be more than just a job description. You can't expect "taxi driver" to cover all the components of what you hold dear. I knew someone who'd been a drummer in a rock band that had *almost* made it; he gave up and become a courier rider. Instead of keeping up the drumming he got rid of everything (he gave me his drum kit) and tried to be as "professional" as possible with matching leathers and a fancy BMW, showing a certain disdain for his former life. He was trying to integrate everything under a *static* definition, a mere job description. And, sadly, as a courier he was less successful than another who rode a battered bike yet was lively and more likable, and who self-identified with being a "world traveler" . . .

The poet, photographer, and businessman Ramsay Wood once told me that identifying as "poet" was much better than being just a "writer." I wasn't sure why but I know now. A poet as an identity vouches a greater connection to the mysterious and valuable—it is a higher-level kind of identity.

It is up to all of us to find a higher-level identity, something that connects and unites all our various elements, something that stops one of our multiple selves murdering the others, something that encourages the growth of all aspects of our personality. The kind of things you micromaster over time will give clues about which higher-level identity is appropriate to you. Merely being aware of it will help you find an identity that works to integrate your life better.

If you overdevelop strength of mind, you may end up despising others—a failure of empathetic development. If you overdevelop caring you may end up stunting someone's ability to stand on their own feet—a failure of perception. But just because an over-development of one aspect is so obviously grotesque doesn't mean we can't try to work on developing ALL aspects.

Glimpse your potential

Having a polymathic worldview might lead you to dabble in many things. Micromastery is the way to turn dabbling into a glimpse of your true and amazing potential. Micromastery is practical polymathy. It's a way to really achieve a dream of doing many things—your personal bucket list, like the wish lists of Clifford Pickover.

It's also a great way into a subject you may eventually choose to master. I have seen people who would be classified as delinquent and incapable of learning anything new walk out of an aikido dojo after a year with a black belt. They started by learning a single move. A micromastery.

I've met people with little formal educational background who have studied a hard foreign language to fluency. They started by entering a language school to find out how to order a meal and a coffee. A micromastery.

Micromastery is about regaining the permission to be interested and involved. In certain eras this philosophy was embraced; how else do we explain the explosions of talent in the "polymathic" phases of history—Islamic Spain, Elizabethan England, Revolutionary America? Once people grasp that their task is to develop their potential *in every direction*, then the world becomes a better, brighter, more enlightened place.

It is the very opposite of any form of narrow-minded fundamentalism that seeks to enslave people to further a worldview. In a small way, micromastery is the first step to becoming truly superhuman.

About the Author

Robert Twigger is a bestselling author, adventure traveler, and lifelong micromaster. His first book, *Angry White Pyjamas*, about a year spent in a Japanese martial arts dojo, won the William Hill Sports Book of the Year Award and the Somerset Maugham Award. He has lectured on risk management, polymathics, and leadership at Oxford Brookes Business School, Oxford University, the Royal College of Art, and to companies including P&G, Maersk shipping, Oracle computing, and SABMiller.

www.roberttwigger.com